SUBJECT TO SOLUTION

SUBJECT TO SOLUTION
Problems in Cuban-U.S. Relations

edited by Wayne S. Smith and
Esteban Morales Dominguez

LYNNE RIENNER PUBLISHERS • BOULDER & LONDON

Published in the United States of America in 1988 by
Lynne Rienner Publishers, Inc.
948 North Street, Boulder, Colorado 80302

and in the United Kingdom by
Lynne Rienner Publishers, Inc.
3 Henrietta Street, Covent Garden, London WC2E 8LU

Library of Congress Cataloging-in-Publication Data
Subject to solution: problems in Cuban-U.S. relations/edited by
  Wayne S. Smith and Esteban Morales
     p.   cm.
    Includes index.
    ISBN 1-55587-127-5 (alk. paper.)
    1. United States—Relations—Cuba. 2. Cuba—Relations—United States
    I. Smith, Wayne S. II. Morales, Esteban
  E183.8.C9S83 1988
  303.4'8273'07291—dc19   88-14162
                                                    CIP

British Library Cataloguing in Publication Data
A Cataloguing in Publication record for this book
is available from the British Library.

Printed and bound in the United States of America

The paper used in this publication meets the requirements of
the American National Standard for Permanence of Paper for
Printed Library Materials Z39.48-1984. ∞

CONTENTS

PART 2   BILATERAL PROBLEMS

FOREWORD

When I first came to the U.S. Senate as a young senator from South Dakota in 1963, I delivered my maiden speech on the theme "Our Castro Fixation vs. the Alliance for Progress." As an aide to President John F. Kennedy in 1961–1962, I had watched the young, new administration blunder into the Bay of Pigs debacle. There did seem to be a "fixation" among Washington policymakers on the challenge posed by Cuban leader Fidel Castro to the power and pride of the United States. That fixation did not cease with the embarrassment over the failed Bay of Pigs invasion.

I argued twenty-five years ago in that first Senate speech that there was no necessity of constant confrontation and hostility between Cuba and the United States. The real enemies of the people of Latin America were poverty and misrule. These were the problems that fed the Castro revolution; they were the problems that created instability and revolutionary ferment in other parts of the southern half of our hemisphere. Diplomatic isolation, economic boycott, and belligerent actions toward Fidel Castro were not the answers to Latin America's problems in the 1960s; they are not the answers now.

Fortunately, there are signs of new perspectives in both Cuba and the United States that augur for better relations between the two countries. The discussions between Cuban and U.S. scholars that led to the essays in this volume underscore both the differences and the antagonism between Havana and Washington, as well as the areas of mutual interest and possible accommodation.

As we watch the steadily improving relations between Washington and the two communist superpowers—the Soviet Union and China—it seems strange that we find it so much more difficult to achieve better relations with Cuba, Angola, and Vietnam. Why is it easier for U.S. policymakers to carry on diplomatic, economic, and cultural relations with the larger communist nations than with the smaller ones? Has the time not come to end this curious double standard?

In a recent interview with the editors of *USA Today*, Fidel Castro observed that the United States is now closer to the Soviet Union than it is to Cuba. "After all," he said, "Reagan and Gorbachev are going to Mars together." This was doubtless a tongue-in-cheek observation by

Castro, but it reminds us that the old Cold War assumptions are breaking down. Cuba can no longer be viewed as a vassal of Moscow—as part of a hostile and relentless international communist monolith.

This book will help us to see that there are a number of areas of mutual interest where Cuba and the United States should be cooperating rather than confronting and undermining each other. If Richard Nixon could enhance his popularity and prestige by opening new doors to China in the 1970s, and if Ronald Reagan can rebuild his damaged public standing after the Iran-*contra* scandals by going to the summit with his Soviet counterpart in the 1980s, perhaps the U.S. president selected in 1988 can make history in the 1990s by ending the confrontational boycott of Cuba.

George McGovern

PREFACE

This book is the result of a series of meetings between U.S. and Cuban scholars organized by the Johns Hopkins University School of Advanced International Studies (SAIS) and the University of Havana's Center of U.S. Studies (CESEU) during 1985, 1986, and 1987. Specialists from both sides were asked to focus on specific bilateral and foreign policy problems that now stand between the two countries, first laying out their own side's positions and basic concerns, and then going on to examine ways in which the U.S. and Cuban governments might try to resolve or reduce each particular problem, should, at some point in the future, they wish to do so. The latter assumption—that is, that both sides have the political will to address the outstanding problems—was basic to the whole undertaking.

This was a first-of-its-kind experiment—the first time that a group of Cubans and U.S. citizens has sat down to discuss in a comprehensive way the whole range of problems between their two countries. It was, of course, an academic exercise—one conducted by scholars, not by diplomats empowered by their governments to negotiate. The essays have no official cachet. For all that, their conclusions are no less revealing.

As will be apparent in several of the chapters that follow, there were sharp disagreements over the genesis and contours of the various problems. Most U.S. specialists, for example, insisted that the U.S. policy of "containment" came in response to Cuba's aggressive efforts to export its revolution to the rest of Latin America. Cuban academics were equally convinced that the exact opposite was the case: that Cuban support for guerrilla groups in the hemisphere was defensive in nature and came only after most other Latin American governments had joined with the United States in a hostile campaign against Cuba. In the same way, U.S. participants held that the Eisenhower administration had not denied Cuba's full right to carry out the agrarian reform law back in 1959 and, indeed, had only taken economic measures against Cuba after the latter started seizing U.S. property without compensation. Cuban participants insisted just as strongly that it was precisely U.S. objections to the agrarian reform law that touched off what amounted to economic warfare between the two countries.

As the meetings progressed, the participants discovered that despite these divergent views and regardless of how the problems between them had originated, it was now possible to envisage solutions to many of them, and especially to those of a bilateral nature. In all cases, it was at least possible to devise ways to reduce the area of disagreement. Participants concluded, therefore, that there was no reason that the various issues that now divide the two countries could not be addressed to the benefit of both. Workable accommodations are available. What is absent is the political decision to sit down and work them out. At least the decision has not been made on the U.S. side. The Cuban government has on several occasions indicated to the United States its willingness to begin such a step-by-step process of problem solving. How far such a process might take the two sides remains undetermined, since on each occasion the United States has rebuffed, or side-stepped, the Cuban government's overtures. At some point, we hope, a U.S. administration will decide that it is time to give diplomacy a try.

Even if that time comes, a cautionary word would be in order. One of the premises of the present exercise is that a sweeping, all-or-nothing "deal" that would resolve all tensions in the relationship is simply not possible. Former Secretary of State Alexander Haig's scenario, in which in return for certain U.S. concessions Cuba would sever its ties with the Soviet Union, abandon Marxism/Leninism, and give up foreign policies objectionable to the United States, was never anything more than so much pie-in-the-sky. No such rearrangement was or is possible, and U.S. policymakers would do well to recognize it. By resolving, or at least reducing, *most* of the issues that now divide them, the United States and Cuba could place their relationship on a more sensible, pragmatic, and mutually productive basis. But even so, they would remain adversaries. Their interests and respective world views are too different for it to be otherwise. The point is, nonetheless, that even adversaries frequently find that their respective interests are better served by accommodation than by confrontation. So, almost certainly, would it be in this case. And that is the principal thesis of this book.

Participants in the meetings were encouraged by the fact that in 1987 one major problem was at last resolved. The need for a migration agreement between the two countries was long-standing but had been amplified by the 1980 Mariel sealift, during which some 125,000 undocumented Cubans were landed on our shores. Talks aimed at reaching such an agreement actually began in 1980 under President Carter, but were not continued by the Reagan administration until late 1984. In December of that year, the two sides signed a fo:mal agreement under which Cuba committed itself to take back a number of excludables and to respect U.S. immigration laws. For its part, the United States agreed to establish a normal flow of immigration from Cuba to the United States. Unfortunately, only five months later, in May of 1985, the United States inaugurated Radio Martí, a station designed to broadcast directly to Cuba. Seeing this as a provocative act inconsistent with the spirit in which the migration agreement had been signed, the Cuban government announced its suspension of that agreement. Almost two more years were to pass before Cuba, in November of 1987, agreed to its resumption. Thus, at long last, one problem between the two countries has been put behind us. The lesson in this is clear: if this one disagreement can be resolved through negotiations, why cannot others?

The present book originally included essays on the migration issue and on how the two sides might resuscitate the 1984 agreement. As this has now been accomplished and immigration is no longer a conflicting issue, those two essays have been removed and will be published separately as occasional papers.

Also, the Cuban side did present a paper on Cuban-Soviet relations in response to the U.S. chapter on the same subject. Unfortunately, the Cuban contribution arrived too late to be included in the book. It has, however, been published separately by SAIS as an occasional paper.

Finally, the reader will note the absence of chapters on the question of human rights. This resulted from the failure of the two sides to agree upon an appropriate context in which to discuss the subject constructively. What one felt ought to be discussed, the other believed to be inappropriate. Thus, there was mutual agreement not to present papers on the issue. The Cuban scholars felt the matter had been pursued in the United States for political rather than humanitarian objectives. U.S. scholars nonetheless emphasized that it is an issue that will inevitably affect relations between the two countries and that, in the real world as opposed to an academic one, must be dealt with. They noted with satisfaction that things are already moving in the right direction, with, beginning in 1978–1979, the large-scale release of those held for crimes of a political nature—a process that has recently been resumed. They expressed full confidence that, in the field of human rights as in foreign policy matters and bilateral issues, both sides could accomplish more through dialogue and engagement than through continued confrontation.

Wayne S. Smith

ACKNOWLEDGMENTS

The Johns Hopkins University School of Advanced International Studies and the University of Havana wish to express their deep appreciation to the Ford Foundation for its generous support of this project. Without its understanding, patience, and financial backing, the series of conferences that gave birth to these essays would not have been possible. At a moment when relations between the United States and Cuba seemed almost beyond repair, the Ford Foundation had the vision to go against the trends and support a project aimed at bringing the two countries closer together. It has the thanks of all of us who were involved in the project.

We also wish to express our gratitude to Coimbra M. Sìrìca, who translated most of the chapters contributed by the Cubans.

ABOUT THE AUTHORS

John Buchanan Marine Lieutenant Colonel Buchanan flew 223 combat missions in Vietnam and then served with Marine ground forces as a regimental air liaison officer. During his twenty-two years of service, he was awarded the Distinguished Flying Cross, the Meritorious Service Medal, fifteen Air Medals, the Navy Commendation Medal, and the Vietnamese Cross of Gallantry, as well as numerous unit citations and campaign ribbons for service in Vietnam. Now retired from the Marine Corps, Lieutenant Colonel Buchanan is a senior staff analyst at the private, non-governmental Center for Defense Information in Washington, D.C.

Carlos Ciaño Zanetti Since 1982, Mr. Ciaño Zanetti has been an assistant professor at the University of Havana and researcher at The Center for the Study of the United States (CESEU). From 1977 to 1982, he was first secretary of the Cuban Mission to the United Nations. He has participated in various international conferences, with presentations concerning the Cuban Revolution and the foreign policy of the United States; some of these papers have been published.

Arnaldo Coro Antich Professor Coro Antich has been a researcher at CESEU since 1982 and is a professor in the Department of Journalism at the University of Havana. He is a specialist in large-scale media, such as international radio broadcasting and satellite communications, and is author of books and essays about international radio broadcasting, the use of satellites in telecommunications, and local broadcasting systems. Since 1983 he has directed the Radio Department of the Center for Study of the Methods of Large Scale Radio Broadcasting (CEMEDIM) of the Journalists Union of Cuba.

Armando Entralgo Gonzalez Dr. Entralgo Gonzalez is an associate professor in the Department of Philosophy and History at the University of Havana and has been titular researcher and director of the Center for African and Mideastern Studies (CEAMO) since 1982. Among his most recent books are *Africa in Difficulties* (Social Sciences, Havana, 1987) and *Panafricanism and African Unity* (Social Sciences, Havana, forthcoming).

Lilia Ferro-Clerico   Dr. Ferro-Clerico is a program associate for the Central American and Caribbean Program at the Johns Hopkins University School of Advanced International Studies (SAIS). Her most recent publication, coauthored with Dr. Riordan Roett, is "The U.S. Response to the Latin American Debt Crisis," in Gerardo Buenos (ed.) *Mexico-Estados Unidos 1986* (El Colegio de Mexico, 1987).

David Gonzalez Lopez   From 1973 to 1979, Mr. Gonzalez Lopez worked as an analyst in international political affairs in the Section of Foreign Agencies of the Executive Committee of the Council of Ministers, and from 1979 to 1982 as first secretary of the Cuban Mission to the United Nations. Since 1983, he has been a researcher associated with CEAMO. He is the author of *Ethiopia: The Counter-Revolutionary Opposition* (Social Sciences, Havana, 1987) and the chapter "The Counter-Revolution in Angola and Mozambique" in the edited volume *Change and Counter-Revolution in Southern Africa* (Social Sciences, Havana, 1987).

Jorge Hernández Martinez   Professor Hernández Martinez has been a professor of sociology and philosophy in the Department of Humanities and the Department of Philosophy and History at the University of Havana and at present gives courses on U.S. foreign policy at the Superior Institute of International Relations (ISRI) and at the University of Havana. He is author of various books on sociological investigations and of numerous articles on the ideology and politics of the United States.

Rafael Hernández Rodriguez   Sr. Hernández Rodriguez is an instructor and researcher on the United States at the Center for the Study of the Americas (CEA).

Kirby Jones   Mr. Jones has visited Cuba more than fifty times in the last twelve years. From 1979 to 1982 he headed Alamar Associates, a Washington-based consulting company, which assisted U.S. firms and organizations to initiate commercial and other contacts with Cuba. He has arranged visits to Cuba for hundreds of corporate representatives. As a CBS special correspondent, he was awarded the Overseas Press Club Citation for Excellence in 1974 for his interview with President Fidel Castro. He is coauthor (with Frank Mankiewicz) of *With Fidel: A Portrait of Castro and Cuba* (Playboy Books, 1975). Mr. Jones was presidential campaign press secretary to George McGovern in 1972. He is currently an officer of an international financial institution.

William M. LeoGrande   Dr. LeoGrande is associate professor of political science in the School of Government and Public Administration at the American University in Washington, D.C. He has been a consultant to a variety of congressional committees, including the National Bipartisan Commission on Central America chaired by former Secretary of State Henry Kissinger. In 1985 and 1986, Dr. LeoGrande served on the staff of the House Democratic Caucus Task Force on Central America. Dr. LeoGrande has written prolifically on Latin American politics and United States foreign policy. In addition to his many articles in journals and newspapers, he is the author of *Cuba's Policy in Africa* (University of California, 1980) and coauthor of *Confronting Revolution: Security Through Diplomacy in Central America* (Pantheon Books, 1986).

Charles William Maynes Currently the editor of *Foreign Policy* magazine, Mr. Maynes is a former Foreign Service officer with service in Laos, Moscow, and the U.S. Mission to the United Nations. From 1973 to 1977, he was secretary of the Carnegie Endowment for International Peace, and from 1977 to 1980, the assistant secretary of state for international organizations.

Esteban Morales Dominguez Professor Morales Dominguez has taught in Cuba for more than twenty-five years. He was dean of the Faculty of Humanities at the University of Havana from 1973 to 1976 and has been the director of the Center of U.S. Studies at the University of Havana since 1979. He has published various articles on themes related to the problems of contemporary capitalism, among which are "The United States: Transnational Militarism and Underdeveloped Countries," 1985; "The Transnational Character of the Militaristic Economy in the United States," 1986; and "Economy and Political Economy in the Context of the Presidential Elections in the United States," 1988. Professor Morales Dominguez is presently cosponsoring (with Wayne Smith) the academic exchange program between CESEU of the University of Havana and SAIS of Johns Hopkins University.

John Spicer Nichols Dr. Nichols is associate professor of communications at Pennsylvania State University. He is the author of *Cuban Mass Media: Organization, Control and Functions* (Journalism Monographs, 1982), and of various articles on the Cuban media in such journals as *World Press* and *Communication Research*. He is also the coauthor (with Lawrence Soley) of *Clandestine Radio Broadcasting* (Praeger, 1987). During ten years studying Cuban media, Dr. Nichols has met with President Fidel Castro and with most of Cuba's top media policymakers and journalists. Most of the research for his essay in this book was conducted while he was a fellow at the Gannett Center for Media Studies at Columbia University.

Hugo M. Pons Duarte Dr. Pons Duarte is a professor in the political economy of capitalism and socialism, Marxist-Leninist philosophy, and international economic relations at the University of Havana. He has published many articles in the national and foreign press dealing with both the Cuban and the international economy. He is the author of *The Decline of a Strategy* (Social Sciences, 1979); *The Critical Balance Sheet of the Industrial Sector in the Latin American Economy* (Social Sciences, 1978); and *Energy Policy, Economic Policy and Development* (Ed. Politica, 1988).

Luis Suárez Salazar Mr. Suárez Salazar is an assistant professor in the Philosophy and History Department of the University of Havana. He has been director of the Center for the Study of the Americas (CEA) since 1984 and director of the magazine *Notebooks About Our America*. He has published many articles on Cuban history and politics and is editor of the book *International Relations in Central America and the Caribbean,* which is now being published in Moscow.

Wayne S. Smith Dr. Smith spent twenty-five years in the U.S. Foreign Service, serving in such posts as Moscow, Havana, and Buenos Aires. When he left the Service in 1982 because of serious disagreements with the Reagan administration's policies, he had been chief of the U.S. Interests Section in Havana for three years and was recognized as the Department of State's leading expert on Cuba. Dr. Smith is now adjunct professor of Latin American studies at the Johns Hopkins University School of Advanced International Studies. In addition to his many articles in journals and newspapers, he is the author of *The Closest of Enemies: A Personal and Diplomatic History of the Castro Years* (W.W. Norton, 1987).

Sanford J. Ungar Mr. Ungar is dean of the School of Communications at The American University in Washington, D.C. His career in print and in journalism spans two decades. Between 1980 and 1983, he was the host of several programs on National Public Radio, including the award-winning "All Things Considered," "Communiqué," and "NPR Dateline." He is also a former managing editor of *Foreign Policy* magazine, a former staff writer for *The Washington Post,* a contributing editor of *Atlantic,* and a long-time contributor to *The Economist* of London. Mr. Ungar has also published five books, among them his best seller, *Africa: The People and Politics of an Emerging Continent* (Simon and Schuster, 1985).

Josefina Vidal Ferreiro Ms. Vidal Ferreiro is a candidate for researcher in The Center for the Study of the United States, with a specialization in international relations. She has studied the interrelation between external factors and North American foreign policy and has dedicated herself in particular to the study of relations between Cuba and the United States.

Part 1

FOREIGN POLICY PROBLEMS

1

THE CUBAN-SOVIET ALLIANCE
Wayne S. Smith

Genesis and Nature of the Cuban-Soviet Alliance

How Cuba came to be so closely associated with Moscow is of less importance than the present nature of that association and its implications for U.S. security. Still, it is worth recalling that it was principally to seek protection from U.S. military power that Cuba turned to the Soviet Union in the first place. This is not to say that U.S. hostility toward Cuba was gratuitous; rather, it was triggered by what the United States perceived to be Cuba's aggressive foreign policy objectives in Latin America. These were best encapsulated by Fidel Castro's vow to turn the Andes into the Sierra Maestra of Latin America and by the Second Declaration of Havana, in 1962, which was a virtual declaration of war against the other governments of the hemisphere. As the United States saw it, Cuba was determined to bring about both the overthrow of those governments and their replacement by revolutionary regimes sympathetic to Cuba. The United States was determined to prevent this, and to use force if necessary. Cuba turned to the Soviet Union as a shield against that force—a shield behind which it could continue to pursue its original objectives.

The resulting situation was more complex than the factors that brought it forth. The Soviet Union, as it turned out, was not particularly interested in turning the Andes into the Sierra Maestra. Rather than encouraging Cuban ambitions in that direction, it sought to restrain them. By the end of the 1960s, moreover, Cuba itself had to come to the conclusion that, in most cases, having good relations with the other Latin American governments made more sense than trying to overthrow them.

1

Meanwhile, Cuba had become a Marxist/Leninist state closely tied to the Soviet Union. This did not, and does not, mean that Cuba is a Soviet puppet. To say that it is, as various U.S. administrations have, is to oversimplify the situation by half. Cuba *is* heavily dependent economically on the Soviet Union and it still looks to Moscow as its principal shield against the United States. Inevitably, this imposes limits on Cuba's freedom of action. As do most small states that lean on a more powerful patron, Cuba must operate within parameters defined by the interests and sensitivities of that patron. It has its interests and objectives—which may differ markedly from those of the Soviet Union—and within the parameters defined by its relationship with Moscow, it pursues its own agenda in its own way. The Cuban-Soviet alliance is a political reality, but that does not mean one can deal with Cuba through Moscow; rather, one must deal directly with Havana.

The U.S. Perception Today of the Cuban-Soviet Alliance

Irrespective of the genesis and specific nature of Cuba's relationship with the Soviet Union, the United States was and is made uncomfortable by that relationship. U.S. administrations may exaggerate, even to themselves—and certainly to the public—the degree of their discomfort, but the fact remains that so long as we live in a world in which the two superpowers confront one another on a global basis, constantly jockeying for military and political advantage, *no* U.S. president can regard a Cuban-Soviet partnership with equanimity. It is not Cuba's socialist system that gives pause; it is the projection of Soviet influence so close under our own guns. The United States can only regard this as potentially threatening, and history lends weight to the concern. In 1962, the threat became real. Despite its assurances to the United States that it had no intention of installing offensive weapons systems in Cuba, the Soviet Union tried to do precisely that, moving secretly to introduce and set up intermediate-range ballistic missiles before they could be detected and challenged by the United States. The result was the 1962 Missile Crisis, which brought the world to the brink of global war.

The Missile Crisis was ended by the 1962 Kennedy-Khrushchev understanding, but Cuba's initial refusal to accept the understanding or to cooperate in allowing the United Nations' supervision of the missile withdrawal—one of the understanding's original provisions—did not make things any easier. Fortunately, Cuba's position has changed over the years. It now accepts the restrictions imposed by the understanding and indicates its willingness to respect them. President Castro has acknowledged that he was wrong and that John F. Kennedy and Nikita Khrushchev did the right thing in 1962 by bringing the world back from the brink of war.

The core of the understanding is found in Nikita Khrushchev's message of October 26, 1962, and in President Kennedy's reply of October 27. Essentially, it is as follows:

1. The Soviet Union would remove its offensive weapons systems from Cuba under United Nations supervision and not reintroduce them.
2. The United States, in return, would pledge not to invade Cuba, and would drop its naval blockade of the island.

As the Cuban government refused to permit on-site United Nations supervision of the missile withdrawal, the Soviet Union took the missiles out as uncovered deck cargo, so that low-flying U.S. planes could count and verify that all had been removed. On a *nolo contendere* basis, this procedure was accepted in lieu of U.N. supervision.

For its part, the United States regards the understanding as operative, has scrupulously respected it, and expects the Soviet Union and Cuba to do the same. So long as it *is* respected, the chances of a United States-Soviet clash over Cuba are much reduced.

Chances of a clash are not, however, dispelled, for both sides may under certain circumstances try to take advantage of the understanding's ambiguities and to test its limits. That was certainly the case in 1970 when the Soviets attempted to establish a facility in Cienfuegos, Cuba, to service their nuclear missile submarines. Even as they did so, they emphasized adherence to the 1962 understanding; apparently, they did not believe the Cienfuegos facility would represent a violation. The United States saw things quite differently. In its view, the operation of nuclear submarines out of Cienfuegos would have been as clearly a violation of the understanding as would have the basing of Soviet bombers at Cuban airfields.

In this instance, the Soviets decided not to make an issue of it; rather, they dismantled the facility and withdrew the submarines. The episode nonetheless illustrates the potential for misunderstanding and conflict *despite* the 1962 understanding.

Another dispute came in 1978 with the provision to the Cuban Air Force of Soviet-made MiG-23 aircraft. Given that the range of these aircraft is somewhat greater than that of the IL-28 bombers, whose withdrawal from Cuba the United States had insisted upon in 1962, and given that one variant of the MiG-23 is capable of carrying nuclear weapons, the United States scrutinized the introduction of the new aircraft as a possible violation of the 1962 understanding. In light of eventual Cuban and Soviet assurances that the MiG-23s turned over to the Cuban Air Force were not nuclear-capable and that there were no nuclear weapons on the island for them to carry—assurances the United States was able to confirm to its own satisfaction—President Carter determined that in fact the introduction of the new aircraft did *not* violate the 1962 understanding.

The interesting thing about this episode was that all sides seemed to agree on where the parameters lay. The Cubans and Soviets did not argue that the introduction of nuclear-capable aircraft would not have violated those parameters; rather, their argument was that such aircraft had not been introduced and that there was no intention to introduce them.

The preceding illustrations are instances in which the Cuban-Soviet relationship resulted in direct military threats to U.S. security that were relevant to the 1962 Kennedy-Khrushchev understanding—or at least in a situation in which such a threat was suspected to exist. There are other instances, however, in which Soviet military presence and activities in Cuba, while not representing either a direct threat to U.S. security or a violation of the 1962 understanding, nonetheless cause—or have caused—problems in U.S. relations with both Cuba and the Soviet Union. An example of this would be the operation of the long-range Bear reconnaissance aircraft from Cuban airfields. These deployments do not in themselves constitute a threat to U.S. cities, and deploying the Bear aircraft to Cuba offers the Soviets only the marginal advantage of being able to keep them over naval surveillance targets for longer periods of time. That in itself poses no particular problem. What does pose a problem is that the Bear reconnaissance aircraft frequently operate near the U.S. coast and they are almost identical in appearance to the Bear bomber. The U.S. air defense system must sometimes go to alert status as these planes approach, and it is never certain whether it is dealing with reconnaissance flights or incoming bombers. This creates tensions and uncertainties which neither side needs and which further strain United States-Cuban relations. Someday, one of the Bears may come too close and get itself shot down, thus causing a major and dangerous incident.

The Soviet intelligence eavesdropping facility in Cuba is another case in point. This violates neither the 1962 understanding nor any precept of international law. The United States itself has had such facilities in countries on the periphery of the Soviet Union. Soviet reaction to this is instructive. It resents the presence of those facilities and regards them as an intrusion. The United States has the same reaction to the facility in Cuba.

Joint Cuban-Soviet military operations abroad are in a separate category. The presence of 30,000 Cuban troops in Angola does not directly threaten U.S. security, nor is there any question of Cuba's legal right to have them there. The troops are in Angola at the request of the Angolan government, which feels itself threatened by South Africa and by UNITA guerrillas supported by South Africa. But while they may have a right to be there and have a justifiable mission, the continued presence of Cuban troops in Angola—and in other African countries—cannot but concern the United States, for it sees in their presence the possible extension of Soviet power and influence. It would be in no one's interest to see Africa turned into a cockpit of great power conflict, yet, since Cuba is the military ally of the Soviet Union, the presence of Cuban expeditionary forces in African states carries us in that direction. The fact that Cuban troops fought in Ethiopia under Soviet command served only to increase that perception and concern.

This is not to suggest that Cuban troops are in Africa to serve Soviet interests or simply because Moscow wishes them to be there. Most observers recognize that the motivation behind their presence is far more complicated than that. Cuba has reasons of its own to have sent the troops. That is understood. But whatever Cuba's purpose, the hard fact remains that as far as the United States is concerned, Cuban policy and actions in Africa *must* be seen against the backdrop of the Cuban-Soviet alliance. The bottom-line question for Washington is to what extent might its position be undermined by and the Soviet position advanced by the presence of Cuban troops in Africa?

Indeed, similar questions must be asked about all aspects of Cuban foreign policy. Were Cuba not the ally of the Soviet Union, the United States might be more relaxed about Cuban activities and policies in, say, Central America. As it is, the United States must assess all of those activities in the context of its global competition with Moscow. Its assessments in this regard, moreover, are likely to be colored by the fact that Cuba's original purpose in turning to the Soviet Union was to advance its revolutionary objectives in Latin America. That being so, the United States is likely to suspect the Cuban-Soviet alliance of being at the root of *present* Cuban policies in the area. That may not be true, but legacies of the past die hard, whether on the Cuban or the U.S. side.

That U.S. suspicions of Cuban foreign policy will be stimulated by Cuba's relationship with Moscow is a hard fact of life, as compelling under Democratic presidents as under Republican, and likely to be muted only by a general relaxation of East-West tensions.

In the absence of such a relaxation, Soviet presence in Cuba would give the United States pause even if it were non-threatening in nature, that is, even if it included no military component. As long as Washington and Moscow are locked in a tense adversarial relationship in which any loss of influence by one is perceived not only as a gain but also as a psychological victory for the other, there will be those who will argue that U.S. tolerance of the Soviet presence in Cuba might in itself be misconstrued as reflecting a loss of will—irrespective of the nature and intent of that presence. This has more to do with perception than reality. The reality is that the United States has suffered no loss of will. When its security and its vital interests are really threatened, as they were in 1962, and as they almost were again in 1970, it will act, and act resolutely, to defend them. Still, as perception rather than reality is often the stuff of politics, the United States cannot be oblivious to the danger that its tolerance of nearby Soviet presence might be misconstrued. This does not mean that it must press things to the point of conflict to counter any such impression, but it does mean that it must carefully weigh its moves in this area and that under foreseeable circumstances, Cuba's relationship with Moscow will be an inhibiting factor in any U.S.-Cuban rapprochement.

The Cuban Perspective

If the United States sees Cuba's relationship with Moscow as potentially threatening to its security, Cuba sees that relationship as protection against U.S. military power. Thus, United States demands that Cuba sever or reduce its military ties with the Soviet Union as a precondition for negotiations with the United States are obviously unrealistic. Cuba can only reduce those ties as it reaches an accommodation with, and feels less threatened by, the United States.

Action to Reduce Tensions

Perhaps the most useful first step the two sides could take toward easing the tensions between them emanating from Cuba's relationship with Moscow would be to recognize that this is at the core of their dispute; that it is a bedrock problem which is likely to be changed only at the margin and only over a considerable period of time, and that both sides would do better to approach it realistically rather than through emotional diatribes. Cuba often complains that its relationship with Moscow is none of Washington's business, that it is a sovereign country and can choose its own friends. True enough; it is a sovereign country and Washington has no juridical right to interfere in its foreign relations. Realistically, however, Cuba must understand that the United States cannot but be interested in anything Moscow does in Cuba or anywhere else in the world and that it has perfectly legitimate security concerns related to the Havana-Moscow axis.

The United States, on the other hand, must understand that while it may object to Havana's relationship with Moscow, the cost of disrupting it would be out of all proportion to the magnitude of the problem. If the United States were willing to put twenty-five divisions in Cuba and then keep half of them there, meanwhile suffering the opprobrium of world public opinion, it might be able to install a government in Havana that would sever ties with Moscow. But in over twenty-five years, no U.S. president has felt the problem warranted such a price. It is unlikely that any will in the future.

Realistically, then, the United States ought to concentrate on modifying those aspects of the Cuban-Soviet alliance that cause it the greatest concerns, not on disrupting the alliance as a whole. Had President Kennedy insisted on the latter in 1962, the result might have been World War III rather than a solution acceptable to all sides. Wisely, he focused on the element in the equation that most directly threatened American security, the positioning in Cuba of offensive weapons systems; and he then brought about their withdrawal.

Both sides must take the other's security concerns and sensitivities into account. Restraint must be mutual. Gratuitous threats and aggressive postures are likely to produce unwanted results—usually, indeed, the exact opposite of what is intended.

A perfect example of this can be seen in the Reagan administration's threats in 1981 to "take it to the source," that is, to attack Cuba as the source of all turmoil in Central America. When asked if the United States intended to bomb, blockade, or invade Cuba, Administration spokesmen replied that no option was excluded.

These threats were gratuitous. The United States had no intention of taking direct military action against Cuba, nor was it necessary to do so. Cuba was not the principal source of the turmoil, and, in any event, had several times indicated to the United States its willingness to discuss the matter, to address U.S. security concerns and to work out a solution acceptable to all sides. When despite these Cuban overtures the United States continued to threaten direct military action, Cuba had little choice, in prudence, but to take those threats seriously. Accordingly, it took steps to bolster its defenses, the most important being the formation of a People's Militia force, which eventually included in its ranks over one million Cuban citizens. In order to arm this huge force, Cuba, during 1981 and 1982, brought in hundreds of thousands of AK-47 assault rifles, and tens of thousands of mortars and machine guns. This of course required the upgrading of its defense agreements with the Soviet Union.

In August of 1981, former Secretary of State Alexander Haig complained of this unprecedented influx of weaponry, which he pointed to as new evidence of close Cuban-Soviet military cooperation. Yet, how had he expected the Cubans to react to his threats to take direct military action against them? By disarming? If so, it was a strange expectation. The reaction he got instead was predictable: An expansion of Cuban-Soviet military ties—the exact opposite of the result the United States sought.

Mutual restraint implies avoidance, not only of gratuitous threats, but also of actions that are provocative or likely to be misinterpreted by the other side. At the nuclear level, uncertainty is always dangerous. An excellent illustration of this was seen in the way the introduction of MiG-23 aircraft was handled by the Cuban side in 1978. Crates known by U.S. intelligence analysts to be associated with Soviet-made MiG-23s appeared on Cuban docks and were then moved to military airfields, apparently for assembly. The United States had no means of determining whether or not the crated planes included nuclear-capable models. Thus, an element of uncertainty was introduced which the United States might have decided to dispel by destroying the planes before they could be assembled. This in turn could have led to a Great-Power confrontation of the first magnitude. In fact, the United States decided that the potential threat was not so compelling that it could not afford to wait until the aircraft were assembled and it had the opportunity to determine whether or not they were nuclear-capable. It eventually concluded that the introduction of MiG-23s did not violate the 1962 understanding. A crisis was avoided, but only because one side calculated that it could react prudently.

The point to be made here is not that Cuba did not have the right to introduce the aircraft, but rather, that their introduction had to be of concern to the United States. Cuba was certainly aware of that. It also had to know that until the United States was assured that the planes were not nuclear-capable, a dangerous ambiguity would exist. It was in Cuba's interest to dispel that ambiguity as quickly as possible, for a miscalculation on the part of the United States might have carried painful consequences for Cuba—as well as raising the possibility of cataclysmic consequences for everyone else. The uncertainty might have been reduced considerably had the Cuban and Soviet sides given assurances *before* the introduction of the planes that they would not be nuclear-capable. After the fact, they did give those assurances, but too late to have avoided a confrontation had the United States decided to react before the aircraft were assembled. The uncertainty, in other words, was allowed to stand well beyond the point of critical mass.

It is not surprising of course that Havana did not give such prior assurances. No side—not the United States, Cuba, or the USSR—has ever done so. No side, in fact has ever even explored the possibility of establishing procedures designed to reduce the ambiguities, and thus the risks, inherent in the introduction of new Soviet weaponry or in other modifications in the Cuban-Soviet military relationship—or, for that matter, in U.S. military moves in the area. It is a possibility worth exploring.

Specific Steps

1. *Avoidance of actions that might be perceived as threatening*: The principal U.S. concern growing out of Cuba's relationship with the Soviet Union is that the latter might use the former as a platform or advance base to threaten the United States. Thus, if tensions are to be reduced, it is crucially important that Cuba—and the Soviet Union—avoid situations or actions that could lend themselves to such an interpretation. Reiteration by Moscow and Havana of their intention to abide by the 1962 understanding can be helpful in this regard, but the main thing is that there be no reason to believe offensive weapons systems might be reintroduced. If there is some doubt on this score, or some possibility of misinterpretation—as there was in the case of the MiG-23s—the matter ought to be thoroughly discussed beforehand between Washington and Havana, and between Washington and Moscow. Ideally, there ought to be some mechanism that would trigger such conversations prior to any major upgrading in Soviet-supplied weapons systems, or in American forces near Cuba.

As suggested, Washington ought to eschew idle threats and aggressive postures and to reiterate its own intention to respect the 1962 understanding. President Reagan's statement in 1983 that the understanding had been "abrogated" was decidedly unhelpful in this regard—even dangerous. Had the Soviets interpreted him to mean the understanding was no longer binding, they might have tested that interpretation by trying to reintroduce offensive weapons systems, the last thing the United States wants. Fortunately, in this instance the Soviets apparently concluded that the President had simply used a poor choice of words and did not act on the assumption that the understanding was no longer binding.

2. *Elimination of unnecessary military activities:* To reduce the perception that the Soviet Union is utilizing its relationship with Cuba to its military advantage, Soviet military activities there should be reduced on a step-by-step basis, with activities that are clearly unrelated to Cuba's defense being eliminated first. These latter activities would include the deployment of Bear reconnaissance aircraft and the operation of the electronic intelligence-gathering facility.

The United States should respond to these steps by eliminating non-essential measures on its side. In the somewhat more relaxed atmosphere implied by Cuban-Soviet willingness to take such steps, the United States could, for example, safely halt SR-71 reconnaissance overflights, given that most of its needs for overhead surveillance can be filled by peripheral and satellite photography.

The United States could also suspend its practice of staging air and naval maneuvers near the Cuban coast. Like the flights of Soviet Bear aircraft near the U.S. coast, these maneuvers result in heightened tensions and the possibility of dangerous confrontations. The only real purpose of such maneuvers, other explanations notwithstanding, is to intimidate the Cubans. As that purpose would be rendered irrelevant by a process of mutual reduction of tensions, the United States could dispense with such maneuvers without in any way endangering its own position.

3. *Stress on Cuban interests:* The strongest U.S. concerns over—and reaction to—Cuban foreign policy result from the perception that it serves Soviet interests more than Cuban. Cuba should avoid actions and statements that reinforce such a perception. Cuba, for example, doubtless had its own reasons for coming to the assistance of Ethiopia in 1978 after that country was invaded by Somalia. Further, given the high degree of coincidence in Cuban and Soviet views on the matter, the cooperation of their forces was natural, and perhaps inevitable. The fact that Cuban forces fought under the overall command of a Soviet general, however, was particularly galling to the United States and was one of the key ingredients in the U.S. conclusion that Cuba was in Ethiopia at Moscow's behest. Had it not been for this conclusion, the damage done to U.S.-Cuban relations by the Ethiopian episode would not have been so severe.

Another clear illustration could be seen in Cuban reaction to the Soviet invasion of Afghanistan. Obviously, Cuban interests were not served by that invasion. On the contrary, they were damaged. Afghanistan was one of the founding members of the Non-Aligned Movement. That Cuba's Soviet allies invaded it just after Cuba had taken over leadership of the movement could not but have been embarrassing to Cuba and caused new challenges to its non-aligned credentials. Certainly the invasion of Afghanistan was instrumental in Cuba's failure to win a seat on the United Nation's Security Council in 1980.

That Cuba did not wish to associate itself with the Soviet action was apparent in the fact that no Cuban leader endorsed it for over a year. Cuban interests, however, would seem to have dictated a policy of more clearly disassociating Cuba from the invasion. This might have been accomplished by voting for the United Nations' resolution that condemned the Soviet action, or by at least *abstaining*. Rather than that, the Cuban Ambassador to the United States gave a lengthy speech in which he said not a word to justify the invasion, but ended by announcing that Cuba would not be placed in the position of voting with the United States and against the Soviet Union; hence, it would cast its vote against the resolution. What he did not explain was why Cuba did not simply abstain. The fact that it did not suggested to many observers that Cuba could not vote its interests even in so clear-cut a case as this, and that it had to follow the Soviet lead. This interpretation infuriated the Cuban government, but it is difficult to see what other interpretation it could have expected to be placed on its negative vote.

If Cuba misplayed its reaction to the invasion of Afghanistan, so did the United States. Cuban and Soviet divergence on the issue was apparent—despite Cuba's vote in the United Nations. One would have expected the United States to emphasize that divergence so as to make the point that even some of Moscow's allies had reservations about its actions. Rather than that, it pretended Soviet and Cuban views on the issue coincided, and it even suggested that punitive actions might be taken against Cuba so as to punish the Soviet Union.

The lesson that both sides might have drawn from the Afghan affair were: (1) That Cuba ought not to vote with the Soviet Union even when its wider interests dictate otherwise, and (2) That even if it does, the United States will usually be better served by looking beyond the surface reaction and fashioning its own policy on the basis of what a realistic assessment suggests Cuba's real interests and inner convictions to be.

Long-Range Scenario: Emphasis on Non-Alignment

Cuba is likely to remain a Marxist/Leninist state, and—at least in our lifetime—it is unlikely to sever its ties with the Soviet Union. One can, however, easily imagine an evolutionary process that would, over time, reduce the degree to which Cuban interests are circumscribed by those of the Soviet Union and reduce the suspicion with which Washington must under present circumstances view Havana's relationship with Moscow.

The principal ingredient in this evolutionary process would be stress on non-alignment. Cuba is a country with something of a dual personality: It is a Soviet ally, but it is also a non-aligned country. It can be both, but it cannot marry the two roles; rather, there is an inherent contradiction between them. Cuba's dilemma has been where to place the stress. In the past, it has tried to have it both ways by carefully balancing the two roles. In fact, however, Cuba's more natural milieu, the forum in which it is likely to accomplish more as a nation, is the Non-Aligned Movement. Thus, in the years ahead, Cuba should, and is likely to, place increasing stress on its non-alignment and less on its ties to Moscow. If this proves to be the case, there would be new reasons to reduce its military links to Moscow. The more active and extensive those links, after all, the greater the challenges to Cuba's non-aligned credentials and the more difficult for it to sustain a major leadership role within the Non-Aligned Movement. The first duty of any government, however, is to assure national survival. Thus, so long as Cuba and the United States are in such a tight confrontational situation, Cuba cannot afford to reduce its military relationship with the Soviet Union, even if reducing it would advance its foreign policy objectives in the Non-Aligned Movement.

One can, then, begin to see the outline of a situation that would be less worrisome to all sides. Ironically, one of the keys to its achievement is the relaxation of tensions between the United States and Cuba.

The United States, certainly, would be more comfortable with a Cuba that placed greater emphasis on its non-alignment and was not so closely tied militarily to the Soviet Union.

Cuba would probably also be more comfortable with such a situation and in a better position to follow its natural destinies in the Non-Aligned Movement. It cannot move in that direction, however, without at least an inchoate *modus vivendi* with the United States.

In the final analysis, even Soviet interests would be furthered by such an outcome. Its influence in Cuba might be reduced, and Cuba, in following a more non-aligned course, might occasionally vote against Moscow in the United Nations, but all that would be balanced by the easing of tensions between Havana and Washington, an outcome that would reduce what must have been a recurring Soviet nightmare of another U.S.-Soviet confrontation over Cuba.

Rather than a zero-sum game in which one side's gain must be the other's loss, the U.S.-Cuban-Soviet equation is one in which all sides would gain from greater Cuban emphasis on non-alignment. Hopefully, some future U.S. administration may understand this and contribute to its realization.

2
ACCOMMODATION OR CONFRONTATION IN CENTRAL AMERICA

2.1 The United States, Cuba, and Central America

Wayne S. Smith

William M. LeoGrande

The United States and Cuba have competing objectives in Central America and back different sides in the conflict there. But are their differences irreconcilable? Might not an accommodation satisfactory to all sides be worked out—given the political will to do so? And is it likely that Cuba—and its Soviet ally—would contribute to such an accommodation? These are the principal questions we will attempt to answer. And if the answers are positive, ought we not conclude that a negotiating option would better serve U.S. purposes in Central America—most especially with respect to Nicaragua?

What Ought U.S. Objectives Be in Central America?

The turmoil and bloodshed which have so afflicted Central America over the past ten years are functions of Central America's need to cast off the old order, characterized by economic underdevelopment, social injustice, and repressive governments, and to replace it with something more attuned to the modern world.

Clearly, it is—and has been—in the interest of the United States to encourage and facilitate the transformation of Central America into a series of modern states that are politically stable, economically vibrant, and moving forward to a future in which there will be a more equitable distribution of goods, justice for all, and popular participation in government. Unfortunately, U.S. policy in the region has not always been shaped by that perception. For years the United States seemed unconcerned over the lack of democracy in Nicaragua, for example; rather, it supported the dictatorship of the Somozas. In Guatemala, it overthrew the progressive government of Jacobo Arbenz in 1954 and then in the years after was happy to cooperate with one military dictatorship after another. El Salvador had one of the most unjust societies in the world, with a few wealthy families taking up most of the land, and, with the help of the military, bloodily suppressing any among the peasant masses who might dare protest or dream of change. The United States accepted that unjust society with complete equanimity. Honduras received virtually no attention. It could remain poverty-stricken forever for all the United States seemed to care.

Clearly, the transition to modernity was in the interest of the United States (whether or not the United States recognized it), and just as clearly, the old order was not likely to give way without a struggle. The bloodier and more protracted that struggle, the more polarized the societies would become and the less likely that moderate, middle-of-the-road governments would fill the vacuum left by the collapse of the old order. Nicaragua was a case in point. As Somoza fled the country in 1979 following a full-scale civil war, there was little doubt as to who would dominate the political landscape in the post-revolutionary period: The Sandinistas, a revolutionary group further to the left than Washington would have preferred, but for whose rise to power Washington bore its full share of responsibility.

The Carter administration made some effort to move away from past policies of support for right wing governments and indifference to poverty and social injustice. It announced a new U.S. interest in human rights and an aversion to dictatorships. Policy actions, as opposed to rhetoric, in fact changed little, but at least when the Sandinista government came to power in Nicaragua in 1979, the Carter administration was sufficiently pragmatic to be willing to work with it, rather than trying to overthrow it as some past administrations would have done (and as the Reagan administration subsequently determined to do).

As the Reagan administration entered office in January of 1981, it faced a difficult task in Central America, but one which was entirely manageable. In El Salvador, a supposedly all-out guerrilla offensive had just been defeated. Skillful use of the leverage provided by our economic and military assistance to the Salvadoran government ought to have enabled the new administration to encourage sweeping reforms and, eventually, a negotiated solution to the war. At least the administration ought to have tried.

The twenty-year guerrilla war continued in Guatelmala, fed more than discouraged by the Guatemalan army's indiscriminate slaughter of tens of thousands of peasants. The military did nonetheless indicate its intention to hold elections and return power—albeit a circumscribed power—to a constitutional government. The United States ought to have sought, through careful diplomacy, to indicate its support for democratic forces, and to expand the parameters within which an elected government would operate. Certainly it ought to have condemned in the strongest terms the slaughter of innocents.

In Honduras, the military was already moving to hold elections and to return power to a civilian government. Honduras, moreover, had managed to hold itself aloof from the turmoil around it. To abandon that course seemed as clearly counterproductive to Honduras' interests as Cambodia's forced involvement in the Vietnamese conflict had been to its destiny. Nor was the former any more necessary than the latter. During 1980 and 1981, the new Nicaraguan government indicated its desire to reduce tensions along the Honduran border and suggested a series of talks to work out ways of doing so. The Sandinistas made it clear that they wanted no trouble with Honduras.

In Nicaragua itself, the Sandinistas, in 1981, acceded to the outgoing Carter administration's demands that they halt assistance to the Salvadoran guerrillas. In doing so, they stressed the value they placed on their relations with the United States and their willingness to negotiate the various areas of disagreement between us. The way was open to constructive diplomacy.[1]

Diplomacy was needed, for the United States had—and has—a number of obvious and legitimate security concerns in Nicaragua. All through their long struggle against Somoza, the Sandinistas counted on one friend: Cuba. Even during the early days, when no one else took them seriously, Cuba offered hospitality and encouragement. The special relationship that developed between Managua and Havana—and Moscow—as soon as the Sandinistas took power was therefore to be expected. This relationship, nonetheless, does represent an East-West component to the problem, and although it may be of secondary importance, it inevitably preoccupies Washington, which has visions of Soviet bases eventually appearing on Nicaraguan soil—or of Nicaragua's acquisition of sophisticated weaponry which might threaten the Panama Canal, nearby sealanes, or even the continental United States. Furthermore, given the adversarial relationship between the United States and the Soviet Union, Washington cannot be comfortable with so many Soviet and Cuban military personnel in Nicaragua.

In view of all this, reasonable U.S. security objectives in Nicaragua might be listed as follows:

(a) To prohibit the establishment of any Soviet military bases or the operation of offensive weapons systems from Nicaraguan territory;

(b) to place limits on the size of the Nicaraguan armed forces and the nature of their armaments;

(c) to bring about the withdrawal of all Soviet bloc military personnel;

(d) to bring an end to any assistance that Nicaragua might still be giving to guerrilla groups in neighboring countries.

There was every reason to believe these objectives might be achieved through negotiations. Although the Soviet Union was willing to provide certain kinds of military equipment (none of which was state of the art), it showed little real interest in Nicaragua, or in the rest of the region. During Soviet General Secretary Mikhail Gorbachev's visit to Washington in December of 1987, he made it clear that Moscow would be willing to severely restrict its military shipments to Nicaragua—possibly to police equipment—provided the U.S. would equally limit its shipments to the other Central American states.[2] The Soviets gave few, if any, arms to the Guatemalan or Salvadoran guerrillas. They refuse to provide hard-currency support to the Sandinista government and, in 1986, even began to cut back on their petroleum shipments to Nicaragua.[3]

Cuba sent military advisors as well as doctors and teachers, but made it perfectly clear that it would not under any circumstances commit troops to Nicaragua's defense. Furthermore, as reflected by Gorbachev's offer mentioned above, both Moscow and Havana emphasized that they were willing to reduce their presence and sharply limit military ties as part of a negotiated regional settlement. For its part, Nicaragua began signalling its preference for a diplomatic process leading to such a settlement as early as 1981.[4] It was the only Central American country to state its readiness to sign the Contadora treaties in September of 1984. The United States blocked those treaties,[5] but regional negotiations continued, and in June of 1986 new drafts were circulated. These new versions, it should be added, addressed all the security concerns originally raised by the United States and would have empowered a verification commission to roam freely over Nicaraguan territory to assure compliance. On June 20, 1986, Nicaragua said it was again prepared to sign, provided the United States would halt the *contra* war against it. The U.S. response came five days later when Congress approved the Reagan administration's request for military assistance to the *contras,* basing itself, ironically, on the rationale that this was the only way to get the Sandinistas to negotiate.

Though one of the salient points of the Arias plan forbade support from extra-regional powers to irregular forces in the area, the Reagan administration refused to comply. Noting that the Arias plan failed to come to grips with the key security issues that concerned the United States, the administration described it as therefore fatally flawed. Such an assertion, however, said more about the administration's own intentions than about the Arias plan. True, the plan did not focus on the externally linked security issues; rather, it concentrated on those things of most pressing importance to the Central Americans themselves, that is, democratic reforms and an end to local conflicts. There was no reason at all, however, that the United States itself could not have taken up the security issues in direct negotiations with Managua—and with Moscow. As we have seen, Gorbachev virtually invited President Reagan to do so. Inexplicably, President Reagan did not respond. Meanwhile, the United States refused also to negotiate with the Sandinistas. This was unfortunate, because the outcome of a process in which the Central Americans concentrated on democratization, while the United States focused on specific security concerns, might have produced results satisfactory to all. For one thing, it might have led to a Nicaragua which, while Marxist in coloration, would have retained democratic forms such as periodic elections and opposition parties, and would not have posed security problems to the United States or to others in the region. Why, one must ask, would that not have been an acceptable outcome from the standpoint of the United States?

What the Reagan Administration's Objectives Are

Acceptable or not, the Reagan administration was not interested in such a solution. It had an ideological agenda of its own, and thus, since 1981, has portrayed the situation in Central America in starkly East-West terms. What we faced, its representatives insisted, was nothing less than Soviet aggression and expansionism articulated through Moscow's Caribbean surrogate, Cuba.[6] Unless we reacted vigorously, the administration warned, the whole area might be swept into Moscow's sphere of influence.

In fact, as we have seen, the Soviet Union has shown little interest in the area. The administration, however, based its policy not on evidence, but on a preconceived contrary assumption. It thus announced that its goal was to "stop communism in its tracks." Accordingly, its objective in Nicaragua, as signalled by the Republican platform in 1980, has been to get rid of the Sandinistas altogether, not to deal with them or simply to restrain them. Only weeks after entering office, President Reagan authorized the CIA to begin operations against the Nicaraguan government, and by the summer of 1981, the Agency was beginning to organize the *contras* around a nucleus of former officers from Somoza's National Guard. From that point forward, the administration's central thrust was to use the *contras* to oust the Sandinistas, or to cause such havoc inside Nicaragua that the whole governmental system would begin to disintegrate.

Since the Contadora process aimed at a regional settlement satisfactory to all sides—and which thus would have left the Sandinistas in power—its objectives and those of the administration were mutually exclusive. The administration not only could not cooperate with the Contadora process, it had to prevent at all cost its successful conclusion. As we have seen, it managed to do this simply by keeping the *contra* war going. So long as the United States would not commit itself to shut down its aid to the *contras* as part of a negotiating process, the Sandinistas could not sign a regional accord that would tie their own hands militarily.

The central fallacy in Reagan's policy is that it leaves the United States in a box. As suggested above, the administration ruled out negotiations, but it couldn't achieve its objectives through its chosen instrument—*contras*—because the latter did not have the military capability to do more than harass the Sandinistas. And harassing them—however viscerally satisfying—does not achieve any discernible U.S. objective. It does not bring about the reduction of Soviet-Cuban military presence. Quite the contrary; the more aid we give the *contras*, the tighter, in reaction, become Managua's martial ties to Moscow and Havana. Nor does it encourage internal liberalization in Nicaragua or encourage the Sandinistas to reduce the size of their own army. Again, just the opposite.

In effect, the administration is left with no workable options at all in Nicaragua. In pressing its *contra* war against Nicaragua, moreover, the administration succeeded in dragging Honduras into the conflict (just as the Nixon administration dragged Cambodia into the Vietnamese war). The *contra* army was organized and trained in Honduran territory and launched its raids into Nicaragua from base camps inside Honduras. This sharply raised border tensions between the two countries. The United States also began to base thousands of U.S. troops in Honduras (under the guise of conducting maneuvers), and built airstrips and other forward basing facilities to be used against Nicaragua. All this military activity strengthened the hand of the Honduran officers against the civilian government and thus impeded rather than facilitated Honduras' transition to full democracy.

In Guatemala, rather than condemning the military government's atrocities, the Reagan administration seemed to condone them—President Reagan at one point in 1982, even said that Ríos Montt, the dictator of the moment, was a fine fellow who had "been given a bum rap by the U.S. media."[7] This, at a time when the dictator's troops were massacring Indians in the highlands. And after the election of a civilian, Vinicio Cerezo, to the presidency in 1985, the administration's surrogate war against Nicaragua and its resulting regional tensions made it more difficult for Cerezo to broaden the parameters of what was tolerated by his own military establishment. Again, as in Honduras, the administration's policy impeded rather than encouraged the transition to democracy.

And finally, in El Salvador, despite some initial successes, the administration's approach left it right where it had started. Military assistance to the Salvadoran army did enable it to fight the guerrillas to a stalemate, rather than losing the war, as the army seemed about to do in 1983. And the holding of elections brought a popular face—José Napoleón Duarte's—to the presidency and improved the image of the government. In order to consolidate these gains, however, it was necessary to press ahead with sweeping economic and social reforms, and to begin talks with the guerrillas in hopes of bringing an end to the fighting. This would have meant a confrontation with the military and the oligarchy, however, and at a time when both were perceived as our allies in the fight against Soviet aggression. The Reagan administration wanted no part of this. It failed, therefore, to use military and economic assistance to El Salvador as leverage in favor of reforms and negotiations. Indeed, it seemed little interested in a negotiated settlement to the civil war. Reforms stagnated, and with them, the image of Duarte. By late 1987, Duarte's political capital was expended and his popularity in tatters. El Salvador's economy was in desperate straits and the guerrillas were again on the rise. With Duarte's term in the presidency almost up, El Salvador's future was ominously uncertain—perhaps even more uncertain than when the Reagan administration had first laid hands on El Salvador, for peace now seemed more distant than ever.

In sum, then, even if one analyzes the situation in terms of the Reagan administration's own objectives in Central America, the policies by which it has tried to achieve them have not been effective. Worse, in pursuing the skewed and unrealistic aims set by its own ideological agenda, the administration has effectively blocked any progress toward the achievement of legitimate U.S. security objectives in the region.

The Cuban Position

If the central U.S. objective has been to get rid of the Sandinista government, Cuba's, by contrast, has been to preserve it. Thus, unlike the United States, Cuba has consistently favored a negotiated settlement in Central America. It also seemed to understand that certain concessions to U.S. security concerns would be prerequisite to peace. Cuba long ago signalled its willingness to make the necessary concessions in cooperation with the Contadora process, or as part of some separate arrangement.

In addition to their public assurances of cooperation with the Contadora process and subsequently with the Arias plan, the Cubans made a number of direct overtures to the United States. In December of 1981, for example, they informed the U.S. government that they had suspended all military shipments to Nicaragua and said they hoped this would improve the atmosphere for a negotiated solution in Central America. The Reagan administration totally ignored this overture and shortly thereafter took new economic measures against Cuba on grounds that the latter was *increasing* its support to subversive groups in Central America. In fact, the United States had no evidence of such an increase. Quite the contrary, it did not even have concrete evidence that Cuban support was continuing.[8]

In March of 1982, Castro indicated to General Vernon Walters that Cuba was prepared to sit down immediately to negotiate all bilateral issues between the two countries. Most issues, he suggested, could be resolved rather easily. Foreign policy issues such as Central America and Africa could be discussed, but, Castro added, solutions in these cases would be much more difficult to come by.[9]

That same month, Castro emphasized to a group of visiting U.S. academics and newsmen that Cuba was ready and willing to discuss *all* issues, foreign policy as well as bilateral, with the United States. Upon its return home, the group reported Castro's statement to the U.S. government. It ignored this overture, as it had ignored Castro's indication to General Walters that Cuba was prepared for serious discussions.

Despite the United States' lack of response, on July 28, 1983, Castro told a group of visiting U.S. newsmen that he was prepared to consider, in consultation with the Nicaraguan government, the removal of all Cuban military personnel from Nicaragua and an arms embargo applied to the entire region—provided the United States would also withdraw its military personnel from the area and respect such an embargo. That particular formula may well have been unacceptable to the Reagan administration, but given the concern it had expressed over Cuban military presence in Nicaragua, the administration might have used this as an opening to begin serious negotiations aimed at working out a formula that *would* have been acceptable. It did not. It initially feigned some interest in the proposal, then dropped any mention of it without ever seriously exploring it with the Cubans.

And so the pattern has continued, with the Cubans pressing for talks with the United States and for a negotiated solution in Central America, and the United States just as assiduously avoiding both. Cuban support for diplomatic processes in Central America does not reflect a more moral or disinterested approach on Cuba's part. Rather, Cuba's principal objective in Central America is the survival of a Sandinista government in Managua—even if it is one severely restrained by a regional agreement and security arrangements, compliance with which the United States would carefully oversee. Negotiations would serve this purpose. For example, the aim of the Contadora process was to produce a regional accord acceptable to *all* parties in Central America—one that accepted the continuation of Sandinista rule in Nicaragua. The Arias plan is also based on the coexistence of the other Central American states with Nicaragua, and so it too is supported by Cuba. The Arias plan, however, does not fully deal with the security issues and thus may not "restrain" Nicaragua in a way satisfactory to the United States. This could be quickly remedied by the direct involvement of the United States in the negotiating process. Indeed, one cannot be overly optimistic regarding the ultimate success of the Arias plan unless the United States *does* become involved. And the question remains: Why should the United States not enter into negotiations to assure its security needs?

Conclusion

U.S. and Cuban objectives in Central America conflict, but need not be irreconcilable. The United States should strive for a Nicaragua that poses no threat to its neighbors, to nearby sealanes, or to the continental United States—a Nicaragua, in other words, constrained by and committed to verifiable international agreements. That outcome is acceptable to Cuba as well. There would be conditions on Nicaragua's internal politics, and Nicaragua would have to renounce any international ambitions, if it ever had any. But the Sandinista government would remain in power (unless at some point voted out) and Nicaraguan sovereignty would be respected.

The key to such an arrangement, however, would be the international agreements defining reciprocal commitments. Since such agreements would serve the interests of both the United States and Cuba—as well as those of the other interested parties—it would make sense for the two to cooperate in bringing such agreements into existence.

As part of such an accommodation, Cuba would have to eschew

any further assistance to guerrillas in Guatemala and El Salvador and agree to keep its hands off the region as a whole. For its part, the United States would, of course, terminate its links to the *contras*. It would also agree not to intervene in the internal affairs of the five countries. And beyond the terms of the agreements themselves, the United States should fashion a policy aimed at encouraging socio-economic reforms and representative government in all five countries—although in the final analysis, the structure of government must be left to each country to decide for itself.

In sum, negotiations that might clear the way for a brighter future in Central America are entirely feasible. It would better serve U.S. interests to pursue such a diplomatic option rather than continuing to use the *contras* as the principal instrument of a policy aimed at getting rid of the Sandinistas. The latter is an approach that has little chance of achieving any of our legitimate objectives; through the former, on the other hand, they might all be attained.

Notes

1. Smith, Wayne S. "Lies About Nicaragua." *Foreign Policy* (June 1987): pp.91–92.

2. As reported in *The Washington Post,* December 16, 1987, p. A-44.

3. Smith, Wayne S. "Seeing Red: U.S. Policy in Latin America." *The Los Angeles Times* (July 26, 1987): V-3.

4. See Smith, "Lies About Nicaragua," 91–92, for a chronology, since 1981, of Nicaraguan offers to negotiate.

5. National Security Council (NSC) memo of October, 1984, which stated exultantly: "We have effectively blocked Contadora efforts to impose a second draft of the Revised Contadora Act."

6. As stated by Secretary of State Haig in February of 1981. Quoted in Smith, Wayne S. "Bringing Diplomacy Back In: A Critique of U.S. Policy in Central America." In *Contadora and the Diplomacy of Peace in Central America,* edited by Bruce Bagley. Boulder: Westview Press, 1987, p.69.

7. Smith, Wayne S. "Reagan Endorsing Double Standard on Human Rights." *The Miami Herald* (January 9, 1984).

8. Smith, Wayne S. *The Closest of Enemies.* New York: W. W. Norton, 1987, p. 235.

9. Haig, Alexander *Caveat: Realism, Reagan and Foreign Policy.* New York: Macmillan Publishing Co., 1984, pp.133–136.

2.2   Cuban Policy Toward Latin America and the Caribbean _____

_____ Luis Suárez Salazar

Cuba and the United States have different and sometimes conflicting views and objectives in Latin America. Those differences are most dramatically visible in Central America. Cuba, however, is committed to peaceful, negotiated solutions whenever possible, and it has over and over again reiterated its support for diplomatic efforts such as the Contadora process and now the Central American peace plan sponsored by President Oscar Arias of Costa Rica. Cuba has also many times offered to discuss Central America with the United States, in hopes that both sides could thus contribute to a peaceful solution. Unfortunately, the United States has always rebuffed such offers. It is to be hoped that at some future time, the United States will adopt a more constructive attitude. When the United States is ready to sit down at the table, Cuba will be waiting.

Historical Problems

One cannot understand Cuba's policies toward Latin America and the Caribbean without some awareness of the historical problems faced by the Cuban Revolution since January 1, 1959. One must also have some appreciation of the environment in which the first socialist democracy in the Western Hemisphere emerged, which conditioned its entry into the international scene.

For more than twenty-five years, Cuba has fought to: (a) Break away from American hegemony; (b) eliminate social inequalities; (c) change the country's political system; and (d) overcome economic underdevelopment.

24

All this has been achieved in the face of continuing U.S. hostility. U.S. elites have attempted—except for brief periods of detente such as the first part of the Carter Administration—to prevent the consolidation of the Revolution and its acceptance as a model for other countries, particularly in Latin America and the Caribbean, which American geopolitical thought has held to be *vital space* for the United States.

Once a new socio-economic order, that is, socialism, had been established at home, the Cuban Revolution launched an active and multidimensional foreign policy which carried to the international scene the democratic aspirations of the new Cuban society: Peace, a new international economic and political order, self-determination, and solidarity among nations.

In a plebiscite held on February 15, 1976, almost 98 percent of those who voted approved the constitutional bases of Cuban foreign policy—a synthesis of international policy principles and goals. This demonstrates the active and direct support of the majority of the Cuban people for the foreign policy developed by the Communist party and the government of Cuba.[1]

The shaping of the Cuban Revolution's international policy has been conditioned by Cuba's peculiar—indeed, *virtually unique*—position on the international stage. Cuba plays roles in many contexts. Geographically close to the United States, its whole national life has been shaped by efforts to defend itself against first the annexationist and then the hegemonic zeal of ruling circles in the United States. Geographically, culturally, and historically, Cuba belongs to the Latin American and Caribbean community of nations, and has close economic, social, and political ties with that region. Cuba's relationship with Africa, on the other hand, is part of its national heritage. As an underdeveloped country it has ties also with the so-called Third World and identifies with the objectives of the Non-Aligned Movement and the Group of 77. And, in spite of the geographical distance that separates them, its political and economic system places Cuba in the community of socialist states gathered around the USSR.

This contextual diversity, incorporated in the theory and practice of Cuban international relations, explains—better than anything else—the universality and global dynamics of Cuban foreign policy,[2] as well as the congruences and differences of opinion between Cuba and other socialist countries, including the USSR.[3] It also points up the fact that Cuban foreign policy has its own singular character. As even some U.S. scholars have noted, "trying to understand Cuba's worldwide activities by looking exclusively—or mainly—to Moscow rather than to Havana is not only insufficient but also foolish."[4]

A marginal and virtually unknown nation before the Revolution,

Cuba has now participated in the highest levels of international activity, overcoming—as many authors acknowledge—its small size and population, as well as its lack of economic resources.

The wide scope of Cuban foreign policy and its international prestige are also explained by the continuity of its goals and the coherence between objectives and actions in various international scenes.

The roots of this continuity and coherence are found in the long-standing and solid popular block which guides this nation-state, and in its political expression, the Communist party. They are also found in the well-known achievements of Cuban society in solving the historical problems that have affected virtually all underdeveloped countries.

The economic, social, and cultural achievements of the Cuban Revolution, as the West German political scientist Robert K. Furtak indicates, contribute to the attainment of Cuban foreign policy goals. In spite of the efforts of successive U.S. administrations, such achievements mark this nation as a "demonstration model," and as proof that "dependency on the United States can be eliminated and social redistribution can become a reality, even in a monoexporting developing country."[5]

Lines of Continuity in Cuba's
Latin American and Caribbean Policy

The major lines of continuity in the purposes and goals of Cuban foreign policy toward Latin America and the Caribbean can be described thus:

1. The Cuban Revolution advocates *Latin Americanism* (Latin American unity) instead of the *Pan-Americanism* put forward by U.S. ruling elites since the end of the nineteenth century.

This was explicitly pointed out in the First and Second Declarations of Havana (1960 and 1962). It was reiterated again in the Cuban Communist Party's (PCC) Program and in the Constitution of the Republic of Cuba, which were approved in 1975 and 1976 respectively.[6] A similar criterion is included in the program of the Cuban Communist Party approved by its Third Congress in February of 1986.[7]

2. This goal of unity, integration, and cooperation with Latin America and the Caribbean challenges U.S. hegemony in the region, and aims at encouraging Latin American and Caribbean nations toward self-sustained development and needed social changes.

Although Cuba's historical experience is proof that socialism is feasible as a valid alternative in overcoming Latin American problems, Cuba has supported, and still supports, all processes of change favoring popular interests, regardless of whether they are socialist or not. This is because of the Cuban political leadership's conviction that the reason socialism is not yet on the agenda of most countries of the region is that the so-called subjective factors of Latin American revolution are not ripe. In addition, Cuba judges that, given their dialectic evolution, democratic and anti-imperialist struggles may eventually contribute to the predominance of socialism in Latin America and the Caribbean.[8]

3. For this reason, since the triumph of the Cuban Revolution its foreign policy has concentrated on promoting radical changes in Latin America's dependent relationship with the United States. The momentum given by Cuba to what Fidel Castro has termed "the struggle against foreign debt" is simply an extension of earlier condemnations of the negative impact imperialist monopolies have had on Latin American development.[9]

Cuba has consistently backed all Latin American assertions of their right to dispose of their natural resources freely and with sovereignty and has supported all diplomatic actions by Latin America and the Third World fostering the establishment of the New International Economic Order.

President Fidel Castro, on the other hand, on various occasions— Chile 1971, the Sixth and Seventh Summits of the Non-Aligned Movement, in 1979 and 1983 respectively—has warned of the negative impact of the foreign debt on regional development.[10]

Since Fidel Castro's first speech before the United Nations in 1960,[11] Cuban foreign policy has insisted on an "inseparable relationship between peace and development" and has asserted the need to reduce expenditures on armaments. Fidel Castro's proposition that Third World—including Latin American and Caribbean—debt could be taken care of by reducing expenditure in armaments by 10 percent simply elaborates this concept, which was also set forth at the U.N. in 1979 and at the Summit of the Non-Aligned Movement held in New Delhi in March 1983.[12]

4. For more than a quarter of a century, Cuban foreign policy has evidenced a clear commitment to the elimination of colonialism in the world, and most particularly in Latin America and the Caribbean. Cuba's continuing support for Puerto Rico's independence, and for the decolonization process in the Caribbean, as well as its endorsement of Belize's independence and of Argentina's claim to sovereignty over the Malvinas Islands, are evidence of this commitment.

5. Cuba has always stated its intention of maintaining relations of

mutual respect with any Latin American government that, regardless of its political, economic, or social system, observes the rules of co-existence among states, abides by the principle of mutual interests, and adopts a policy of reciprocity toward Cuba. Cuban-Mexican relations are based on these criteria. The breakdown of relations with almost all Latin American governments in the first half of the 1960s cannot be attributed to Cuba, but rather to the fact that these countries acceded to U.S. pressures to join in the blockade of Cuba. Cuba's *selective policy* toward democratically elected governments in the Western Hemisphere during the period of its re-emergence on the international scene (1959–1962) continued in the 1970s in the form of its willingness to re-establish relations with all those Latin American countries that broke with U.S. policy toward Cuba.

6. Cuba has consistently condemned foreign intervention in the domestic affairs of Latin American countries. Its criticism of the U.S. intervention in Santo Domingo (1965) followed the same rationale as criticism of U.S. military intervention in Grenada (1983).[13]

7. Likewise, Cuba has denounced military dictatorships in the region and has backed all political and social movements that challenged them—regardless of their class origins or bias.

8. Historically, the Cuban government has also expressed solidarity with those Latin American nations and their political representatives who have been committed to reform programs and to ending Latin American dependency. Such solidarity has been shaped by the specific circumstances of each country, the development level of social and political actors interested in programs of change, and by the attitude of their governments toward Cuba.

Conventionally, Cuba's solidarity with Latin American nations is thought of in terms of the military assistance it has offered to various revolutionary organizations or governments in the region. This view, however, disregards the predominantly civic nature of assistance offered to those Latin American and Caribbean governments that are regarded by Cuba as anti-imperialist and progressive. Also ignored is humanitarian assistance given to nations of the region affected by natural disasters—even in cases where political, state, or diplomatic relations did not exist with those countries. An example of this was the public health assistance provided to Peru on the occasion of the 1970 earthquake. Another was aid of the same nature given to Nicaragua during the earthquake of 1973, when that country was still governed—badly—by the tyranny of Anastasio Somoza.

9. Independently of the clearly anti-imperialist nature of Cuban foreign policy and of its challenging attitude toward the United States,

the Cuban government has always been willing to seek negotiated political solutions to international conflicts. In this respect, Cuba's attitude toward the bilateral dispute with the United States is consistent with Cuba's position regarding the Central American conflict, and in particular with its support for any negotiated political solution which is respectful of the sovereignty and self-determination of the countries of that region.[14]

This will to negotiate was clearly reiterated by President Fidel Castro in his Central Report to the 3rd Congress of the Communist Party held in February, 1986. There he clearly said that Cuba has participated in the search for a negotiated solution to the Central American conflict and will continue to do so. Such a solution, however, would have to involve a commitment by the U.S. government to give up any aggressive actions against the Nicaraguan people, and would have to take into account the need for negotiated solutions to the civil wars in El Salvador and Guatemala. In addition, in this same document, President Castro reiterated Cuba's disposition to reach agreements with the United States "that are reasonable for both parties, regardless of the ideological abyss that separates our governments." The migration agreement, signed by Cuba and the United States in 1984, was an example of Cuba's willingness to reach negotiated solutions "whenever we are respected as a sovereign, equal nation, without the absurd and intolerable interventionist pretensions which have, in general terms, characterized American policy toward Cuba, for more than twenty-five years."[15]

This reaffirmation of Cuban policy was consistent with contacts initiated in 1963 by an envoy of the late U.S. President John F. Kennedy, who sought some less hostile arrangement with the Cuban government. It was also consistent with Cuba's receptiveness to similar proposals made by Henry Kissinger in 1974, when secret negotiations between the two governments took place and a review of Cuban-U.S. relations was initiated. Finally, it was consistent with Cuba's constructive attitude toward the Carter administration's policy of detente, and even with discussions held between Cuban Vice President Carlos Rafael Rodríguez and U.S. Secretary of State Alexander Haig in 1981. This last meeting was followed by discussions between the current U.S. Ambassador to the U.N., Vernon Walters, and President Fidel Castro himself. However, as the former chief of the U.S. Interests Section, Wayne Smith, has pointed out, the Reagan administration systematically ignored or rejected Havana's offers for negotiation and dialogue.[16]

Cuba's disposition to seek negotiated solutions to international conflicts—particularly to those with a more or less direct impact on

Cuba—is based on the belief that the struggle for peace, in all its manifestations, constitutes an essential element of Cuban foreign policy. "The fact that there is an inevitable contradiction between socialism and capitalism," says Vice President Carlos Rafael Rodríguez, "does not mean that this contradiction has to be resolved through armed conflict. . . . Therefore, we Cuban communists consider the contribution to the victory of socialism to be perfectly compatible—even *necessarily compatible*—with peaceful coexistence."[17]

The major lines of continuity in Cuban foreign policy toward Latin America and the Caribbean, mentioned previously, are rooted in Cuban history, traditions, and political thought. As he was dying on the battlefield in the war against Spanish colonialism, the hero of Cuban Independence, José Martí, stated his conviction that the independence of Cuba and Puerto Rico would prevent the United States from reaching out to grasp the other American Republics. Martí had earlier named these Republics *Our America* to distinguish them from the *Other America* (the United States), which scorns and looks down on the first. He had exhorted the countries south of the Rio Bravo to offer a "unanimous and virile" response to a "secular and confessed policy of predominance by a powerful and ambitious neighbor who has never supported these countries, and has only gone to them to prevent them from expanding . . . or to seize their territory . . . or to intimidate them . . . or to oblige them to buy what remains unsold and unite under its domain."[18]

Martí's political legacy was cultivated by every sector of Cuban society which questioned Cuba's dependency on the United States, and was used by Fidel Castro as the ideological platform for the program of change which united the nation against the dictatorship of Fulgencio Batista (1952–1958).

This explains why the struggle against colonialism, and for Latin American unity against U.S. domination, became the national policy of the Cuban Revolution from its inception. It also explains why one of the Revolution's major objectives is to obtain recognition that Cuba "aspires to become integrated with Latin American and Caribbean countries free from external domination and internal oppression, in a community of nations joined by historical traditions and a common struggle against colonialism, neocolonialism and imperialism, with the purpose of achieving domestic and social progress."[19]

These lines from the Cuban Constitution are simply another way of expressing the sentiment articulated by Fidel Castro during his trial following the attack on the Moncada Barracks in 1953: "Cuba must be a bastion of freedom and not a shameful link to despotism!"[20]

Two Policies Contrasted

Over more than twenty-five years, the coherence of Cuba's international policy has undoubtedly contributed to the erosion of the diplomatic, economic and political blockade imposed by the United States against this small island. The central argument used by the United States to mobilize support for the policy of roll-back or containment of the Cuban Revolution was that changes taking place in Cuba were *dangerous* for the security and stability of the Hemisphere. This was especially so, according to the United States, because Cuba tried to export its revolution with the support of extra-hemispheric elements. In spite of the intensity of this campaign, its effectiveness with most governments of the Hemisphere was short-lived—approximately ten years. Today most of the arguments in that campaign are seen to have been false. How can one explain, for example, the fact that armed struggle in Latin America became generalized after, and not before, most Latin American governments broke relations with Cuba? And how to justify the fact that the United States maintains diplomatic relations with other socialist countries which have a closer relationship to the USSR than does Cuba?

These questions are not easy to answer even for U.S. decision-makers themselves. Much less so since Cuba currently has diplomatic and trade relations or maintains different degrees of communications with all South American countries, save Chile and Paraguay. In the so-called Caribbean Basin, it has various levels of relations with Panama, Nicaragua, Trinidad and Tobago, Guyana, Barbados and the Bahamas. In North America, it has maintained stable and fruitful relations with Mexico and Canada. What danger, then, does the export of the Castro-Communist revolution represent for most Latin American and Caribbean countries? Apparently, it is not perceived by them as sufficient to inhibit relations with Cuba. Furthermore, Cuba participates in virtually every existing Latin American organization and in the regional groups within various international fora. In addition, it can be empirically proven that Cuba's foreign policy positions have found increasing acceptance in the rest of the Hemisphere. There is a growing sentiment for Latin American unity, and even in Canada, growing acceptance of the need to redress the inequitable and asymmetrical relationships with the United States. This tends to legitimize the postulates advocated by the Cuban government since January 1959. In other words, as Rafael Hernández has correctly stated: "The alleged export of revolution seems to have earned Cuba more appreciation in the Third World than the U.S. has achieved with its policy of isolationism."[21] Rather, as Cuban Vice Minister Ricardo Alarcón says:

"In the effort to isolate Cuba, it is the instigators of the blockade who have been isolated."[22]

Obviously, there are deeper causes than the blockade for growing U.S. isolation from Latin America and the Caribbean. One of the main reasons is that the United States today does not offer, as it sometimes did in the past (the New Deal, the Alliance for Progress), any positive program or proposed solution to the economic, social, political, and diplomatic problems between the United States and its neighbors.[23]

Profound economic and social changes have taken place in Latin America and the Caribbean since the beginning of the 1980s; yet U.S. ruling circles—particularly the Reagan Administration—seem to have rejected those changes. This is especially critical in Central America, where the triumph of the Sandinista Revolution and the popular uprisings in El Salvador and Guatemala pose a direct challenge to traditional U.S. hegemony in the region, given that the United States was so closely identified with the status quo in those countries—as even the Kissinger Report was compelled to recognize.[24]

Faced with these two situations, various Latin American countries have called for negotiated political solutions. Although not a direct participant in either of these two situations, Cuba has advocated solutions which coincide—as in the case of the Central American crisis—or which tend increasingly to coincide—in the case of the foreign debt—with those proposed by other major regional actors. Cuba stressed its full support for the Contadora process and its willingness to cooperate with and scrupulously respect any arrangements that resulted from that process. It has taken the same position with respect to the Arias Plan. Meanwhile, the current U.S. administration refuses to heed the calls for negotiated solutions. Aid to the Nicaraguan *contras* is simply a reaffirmation of the decision to roll back the Sandinista Revolution and to prevent a negotiated solution. On the other hand, military aid given to the Salvadoran government not only has failed to achieve the goal of destroying the FMLN-FDR, but has also hampered any chances for internal negotiations and has exacerbated the anti-American feelings of broad sectors of Salvadoran society. It might seem that once again the ways and means selected by the United States serve—as they did in the Cuban case—as a self-fulfilling prophecy.

This is also the case with the Latin American economic crisis and its most serious aspect, the foreign debt. The U.S. government has a decidedly myopic view of this issue—one which fails to recognize that the lack of a solution to the foreign debt problem jeopardizes any possibility of economic development. This could cause—as Fidel Castro has said—uncontrollable social outbursts and even revolutionary changes in some Latin American countries.[25]

In the Bipartisan Commission Report on Central America, Henry Kissinger recognizes that, "peace is needed in order to have progress. Security is needed to have peace: progress is needed for peace to be long-lasting." But this truism is ignored by the Reagan Administration in its approach to the growing Latin American debt.[26]

Is it not possible to find new avenues to better understanding between the Northern and Southern regions of the Hemisphere, including Cuba? Or are we condemned to accept the perverse rationale that changes in U.S. foreign policy are only possible after major tragedies occur, such as: The financial crisis of 1930, or the Vietnam War, or the October Missile Crisis when the world came to the brink of a devastating nuclear exchange?

A sense of political realism leads one to believe that confrontation could be replaced by negotiations among the United States, Latin America and the Caribbean, including Cuba, on the basis of mutual respect, self-determination and the full right to choose their respective roads to development. This concept is rooted in the theory and practice of Cuban foreign policy toward Latin America and the Caribbean. And that is why the ideas expressed by President Fidel Castro on February 19, 1959 remain essentially in force: "The government of Cuba does not want to be the enemy of the United States, nor of any other government in the world. . . . We are now a completely sovereign and free nation and as a free and sovereign nation we are entitled to pursue our own political destinies, just as the United States does . . ."[27]

Is it not time for the United States and Cuba to sit down to discuss their differences like the mature, rational nations they in fact are?

Notes

1. 5,473,534 citizens voted in favor of the Constitution of the Republic of Cuba and 54,070 voted against it. 2 percent of those who could vote, abstained. For a reading of the constitutional basis of the Republic of Cuba's foreign policy, see "Constitución de la República de Cuba." *Edición DOR* (1976), pp.17–20.

2. Frequently, studies of the Cuban Revolution's foreign policy explain it as an appendix of Soviet foreign policy. Lately the tendency to do this has been dropped both by the U.S. academic community and, for all their rhetoric, by some U.S. policy makers in charge of Cuban policy. See Skoug, Kenneth: Speech given on December 17, 1984, in the "Face to Face" program, Carnegie Endowment.

3. For an official presentation of this subject see Rodríguez, Carlos Rafael. "Strategic Bases of the Cuban Revolution's Foreign Policy," *Revista*

Cuba Socialista, no.1 (Dec. 1981), pp.10–83.

4. Dominguez, Jorge L. "Cuba: Charismatic Communism." U.S.: *Problemas Internacionales,* (Sept.–Oct. 1985), pp.103–108.

5. Furtak, Robert K. "Cuba: A Quarter of a Century of Revolutionary Foreign Policy." Mexico: *Foro Internacional,* vol. 25, no. 100 (April–June 1985), pp.10–33.

6. Program of the Cuban Communist Party. "Thesis and Resolutions." *Ediciones DOR.* Havana: (1976) p.107. For the Constitution of the Republic of Cuba, see "Constitución de la República de Cuba." *Ediciones DOR* (1976), pp.17–60.

7. Proposed Program of the Cuban Communist Party. *Revista Bohemia,* no.24, 78th Year (June 13, 1986), pp.47–49.

8. Rodriguez, Carlos Rafael. "Twenty five Years Since the Victory of Girón Beach and the Declaration of the Socialist Nature of the Cuban Revolution." *Cuba Socialista* (March–April 1986), no.20, p.25.

9. Castro, Fidel. Interview with Mexican Newspaper *Excelsior, Editora Politica,* Havana, March 2, 1985. Also, see "The Settlement of the Foreign Debt or the Political Death of Democratic Processes in the Hemisphere," interview of Fidel Castro by Congressman Marvin Dymally and academician Jeffrey Elliot, on March 29, 1985, *Impresora del Palacio de las Convenciones,* Havana, Cuba.

10. Castro, Fidel. "The Foreign Debt." Selection of Issues, Feb.–Sept. 1985 by Martha Harnecker. The Cuban State Council Publications Office, Havana, 1985, pp.168–176.

11. Castro, Fidel. Speech delivered during the 15th Session of the UN General Assembly, 26 September 1960; text in *The Thought of Fidel Castro* (Havana: Editora Politica, 1983) pp.122–146.

12. Castro, Fidel. "The Third World Economic and Social Crisis." *Editora Politica* (1983), pp.221–222.

13. Castro, Fidel. "Eulogy for the Cuban martyrs during the U.S. intervention in Grenada." *Granma* (November 15, 1983), pp.2–3.

14. For a detailed analysis of Cuban policy on the Central American crisis, see Valdés, Juan. "Cuba and the Central American Crisis." *Cuadernos de Nuestra América,* vol.1, no.2, Published by Center of Studies on the Americas, Havana, Cuba. (July–December 1984), pp.122–153.

15. Castro, Fidel. "Report to the 3rd Congress of the CCP." *Revista Bohemia* (February 14, 1986), no.7, pp.77–78 and 83.

16. Quoted in Lofredo, Gino. "Cuba-United States. 25 years of Tense Relations." *Cuadernos del Tercer Mundo,* Mexico (Nov. 1985), pp.44–50.

17. Rodríguez, Carlos Rafael. "Strategic Bases, the Cuban Revolution's Foreign Policy." *Cuba Socialista* (March–April 1986) no.20.

18. Benítez, José. "Martí and the United States." *Editora Politica* Havana, 1983, pp.1–7.

19. "Constitución de la República de Cuba," pp.17–20.

20. Castro, Fidel, "History will Absolve Me." *Ediciones Populares.* Cuban National Press, 1961, p.59.

21. Hernández, Rafael. "Prospect for Negotiation between the U.S. and Cuba." U.S.: LULAC, forthcoming.

22. Alarcón, Ricardo. "Theory and Practice of Latin American Foreign Policy," (Bogotá: University of the Andes, 1983), pp.449–459.

23. In this respect, see "Latin America-United States: The Political and Economic Agendas." *Cuadernos Semestrales CIDE,* no.14 and 15, Mexico (first and second semesters of 1984).

24. "The Bipartisan Commission Report on Central America." *La Nación.* Costa Rica: (January 13, 1984), pp.10–20.

25. Castro, Fidel. "Fidel and Religion (Conversation with Frey Beto)." State Council Publications Office, Havana, 1985.

26. Suárez Salazar, Luis and Casanova Alfonso. "On the Reagan Corolary and Kissinger Report." *Cuba Socialista,* no.1 (June–August 1984), pp.41–76.

27. Castro, Fidel. "The Thought of Fidel Castro," op. cit, p. 18.

3

DISAGREEMENTS IN AFRICA

3.1   Cuba, the United States, and Africa

Sanford J. Ungar

It has become increasingly apparent in recent years that the substantial Cuban presence in Africa is a complicating factor in both U.S.-African and U.S.-Cuban relations. It is beyond the scope of this chapter to probe the fundamental political (and perhaps psychological) motivations that cause the U.S. government—and its people—to give evidence of a distinct Cubaphobia. Whatever the underlying causes, Africa seems second only to Central America as an arena in which the symptoms of this phobia are especially noticeable—and in which Cuba, as a Soviet ally, is genuinely resented and feared.

On a continent where U.S. foreign policy is at best unsophisticated and contradictory, and at worst heavy-handed and self-defeating, the official U.S. attitude toward particular governments is all too often based on those governments' positions concerning the Cuban role in Africa, especially in Angola. So strong are U.S. feelings on the issue that African leaders who openly express disapproval of Cuba's role may well be rewarded with U.S. economic and military assistance and those who demonstrate approval of, or even indifference toward, Cuban involvement in Africa, often find their relationship with Washington compromised. This is true notwithstanding the widely held position of African governments that the presence of Cuban troops in Angola is a matter to be handled in those two countries' bilateral relations, rather than in negotiations with the United States.

What is the origin of this extraordinary standoff between the capitalist superpower and a Marxist Caribbean island state over distant events on the least-developed continent in the world?

Few U.S. citizens are aware of the strong cultural ties between Cuba and Africa. Unless they have visited Cuba (and not many have done so during the past twenty-five years), U.S. policymakers do not recognize that the Afro-Cuban heritage has been exalted in Cuban politics and has played a significant role in the formulation of post-revolutionary Cuban foreign policy. Indeed, it is easily overlooked, or forgotten, that Cuba has actually been active in Africa since the early 1960s—as a minor supporter of the Algerian side in the first Algerian-Moroccan war in 1963, as a force in the attempt to construct an anti-Western guerrilla movement in the Belgian Congo (now Zaire), and as an early backer of the Marxist government in Congo-Brazzaville. Isolated in the Western Hemisphere by the Organization of American States, Cuba sought out kindred spirits in the developing world; it found them especially in Africa, including Ben Bella's Algeria and Kwame Nkrumah's Ghana. Che Guevara went on his famous, and eventually fatal, expedition to Bolivia only after failing to succeed militarily in the Congo.[1]

However unaware they might have been of the original motivations for Cuba's attention to Africa and of the early steps taken there by Fidel Castro, U.S. citizens could certainly not fail to notice the substantial and sustained Cuban presence in Angola dating from the mid-1970s and Havana's intervention in the Horn of Africa a few years later. It may be argued that the Cuban commitment to the MPLA forces in 1975, at the time of Angolan independence and in the midst of the country's civil war, was merely an extension of the assistance that Guevara had given to the Marxist-oriented liberation movements in the various Portuguese colonies ten years earlier; but in U.S. eyes, there was a major difference.

The fact is that the Cubans, who seemingly began to pour into Africa at this point, were not just political advisers, military instructors, teachers, and doctors—all of whom might have made the United States nervous, but would not have been seen as a meaningful threat to Western interests. For the first time, the Cubans sent combat troops overseas. This more ambitious role became possible largely because of the greater closeness between Cuba and the Soviet Union that had been achieved in the early 1970s, exhibited particularly in matters of foreign policy—a closeness brought about in part by U.S. hostility toward Cuba.

None of this is to say that the Cubans were somehow "ordered" into Angola by Moscow, as is often emotionally and simplistically claimed by conservative U.S. politicians now sponsoring military aid for the guerrillas of the allegedly pro-Western National Union for the Total Independence of Angola (UNITA), led by Jonas Savimbi. Castro has always insisted, and independent evidence seems to confirm, that in the case of Angola, the Cubans made their own decision to intervene. Indeed, they actually seemed at the time far more willing than the Soviets to risk a confrontation with the West over southern Africa.[2]

Whatever the subtleties, however, they have not loomed large in the U.S. evaluation of Cuba's actions, under either Democratic or Republican administrations. Easily ignored was the fact that the Cubans had actually done some good in Angola, and elsewhere in Africa, and that in most cases they were welcomed and well-liked by Africans as people who brought knowledge and experience relevant to Africa's economic development. Viewed from Washington—a view that has been influenced and exaggerated in recent years by the close relationship between the Reagan administration and the government in Pretoria, and thus, indirectly, by South African paranoia—the Cubans in Angola are perceived to be carrying out policies that explicitly advance the political and military interests of the Soviet Union. The Cubans have now been defined, through the policy of "linkage" as the primary stumbling block to an internationally acceptable formula for the independence of Namibia. And, perhaps most fearsome in some circles, they have been seen to be gaining combat experience in Africa that could one day prove useful to them in other encounters in Central America and the Caribbean.

The latter point—the notion that Cuba has used Africa as a training ground for future military adventures—was exacerbated by the sudden escalation of Cuban involvement in the Horn of Africa in late 1977 and early 1978. Here it could be argued that the Cubans were acting more obviously and directly as Soviet proxies, terminating their relationship with Somalia and backing the radical military regime of Mengistu Haile Mariam in Ethiopia virtually in tandem with the Kremlin. When Cuban troops and their commanders fought (and died) side-by-side with the Ethiopians to repulse an invasion in the Ogaden desert by Somalia— with the Soviet military actually transporting the forces and participating in strategic planning—the perception of Cuban adventurism grew even stronger in Washington.[3] The insult was perhaps all the harder for U.S. citizens to take, given the influence the United States had once enjoyed in Ethiopia during the reign of Emperor Haile Selassie, but had now lost.

There were, to be sure, mitigating factors that might have been considered in evaluating the Cuban role in the Horn of Africa, just as there had been in Angola: The intransigence of Somali leader Mohammed Siad Barre (soon to become a U.S. ally), who insisted on including the Ogaden as part of his dream of a "greater Somalia" that would eventually encompass Djibouti and a substantial part of Kenya as well; the general Cuban reluctance to participate in the brutal

Ethiopian war against separatists in Eritrea; and the willingness of the Cubans to withdraw some of their forces as soon as the fighting had died down and Ethiopian security had been restored in the Ogaden. But those factors offered scant solace to the U.S. government, which perceived Cuban complicity in the creation of an "arc of crisis" extending across Africa and the Persian Gulf and into South Asia. At the same time, disillusionment was spreading over President Jimmy Carter's human-rights-oriented foreign policy. As Zbigniew Brzezinski, Carter's national security adviser, said at the time, detente (and, he might have added, the U.S. desire to achieve a rapprochement with Castro's Cuba) "lay buried in the sands of the Ogaden."

Just as U.S. citizens often demonstrate a lack of understanding of the origins and the history of Cuban involvement in Africa, many Cubans tend to underestimate the strength and the depth of U.S. feelings on this issue. That is equally unfortunate. Although there is room for differences of nuance and emphasis, no U.S. president of either party could dare to ignore those feelings without committing political suicide. Nor could any president, realistically speaking, be indifferent to the continuing presence of tens of thousands of troops belonging to an ally of his Soviet adversary in an area as unstable and as fragile as southern Africa. In the final analysis, it does not matter how they got there, why they stay, or who else is behaving badly in the region—the Cuban troops in Africa are seen as a threat to U.S. strategic interests.

Certainly it can be said that Cuba's presence in Africa remains a complicating factor in U.S.-Cuban relations, or in the lack of such relations. Among the various efforts to improve the atmosphere between Washington and Havana in the past decade, many have foundered on the faraway shores of Africa. While it should be acknowledged that a vast percentage of U.S. citizens would not be able to find Angola on a map of the world, a surprising number of them, having heard so much discussion of the matter, would probably know nonetheless that there are tens of thousands of Cubans there. The typical U.S. citizen, having become convinced that these Cubans in Angola are "up to no good," would argue vehemently that they must leave—or at least begin to leave—before Cuban and U.S. officials can discuss any other issues of substance.

To demonstrate the extent to which the controversy over Cuba's role in Africa has permeated U.S. politics, as well as U.S. foreign policy, it is useful to consider the perspective of various political tendencies: For the right wing—which, it should be remembered, now holds power in the Executive Branch, if not in Congress—Cuba is in Africa strictly as a surrogate and client state of the Soviet Union. No distinction is made between Soviet and Cuban goals, behavior, and methods on the continent; nor is any drawn between the Cuban soldiers and the other Cubans working in Africa. In official U.S. rhetoric and in unofficial statements alike, the Soviet (and therefore Cuban) purpose in Africa is defined as the cultivation and strengthening of Marxist forces in a manner that excludes others, often brutally. And this, in turn, is widely perceived to be inimical—perhaps even directly threatening—to U.S. national security.

Political conservatives see the Soviet-Cuban "problem" manifesting itself in a variety of ways across the African map, and they generally believe it is directly related to the issue of Soviet-Cuban "subversion" elsewhere—for example, in Central America. Their attitude is reinforced by the presence of a strong strain of conservatism that exists among U.S. diplomats serving in Latin America, whose influence in these matters is far greater than that of U.S. foreign service officers working in Africa.

In Angola, the conservatives believe, Cuba is propping up an unpopular, ineffective MPLA government that could not survive the challenge of Jonas Savimbi's purportedly pro-Western UNITA forces without massive aid from Havana, and they suspect the Cubans of participating directly in the war against UNITA in the Angolan countryside. In Ethiopia, they argue, Cuba helped entrench and reinforce one of the most unsavory regimes in the world. And elsewhere in Africa, they fear, smaller Cuban contingents are sowing subversion and waiting for opportunities to manipulate conditions in order to put their own friends in power. This is Thomas O. Enders, then Assistant Secretary of State for Inter-American Affairs, talking about Cuba before a congressional subcommittee in December 1982:

> Cuba is at once a would-be foreign policy giant ceaselessly projecting political-military influence far beyond its borders and an economic dwarf which for years has shown itself incapable of providing material progress for its own people. . . . Cuba's objectives in Africa are to capitalize on general African opposition to the Republic of South Africa to compete with the United States on a favorable ideological battlefield while enhancing Cuba's stature and promoting the establishment of pro-Soviet, pro-Cuban regimes in the region. The emphasis in Africa is part of Cuba's effort to become an actor on the world stage and reduce its diplomatic isolation. Cuban activities in the region are based in part on Cuba's revolutionary internationalist ideology but also serve Soviet interest.[4]

Despite the evidence of a substantial Cuban pullout from Ethiopia (for reasons that have never been completely appreciated among some U.S. officials and academics), the conservatives do not believe that

Cuba wants or intends to reduce its presence in Angola, and they distrust suggestions by the Angolan government that it would be willing to send some of the Cubans home and move others to the northern part of their country as part of a deal in exchange for South African withdrawal from Angola and Namibia. The conservatives perceive a long-range Cuban entrenchment in Angola as a factor that necessarily complicates the situation in Namibia and South Africa, rather than the other way around. While most U.S. conservatives, once they become more familiar with the situation in South Africa, are not overtly sympathetic to the apartheid regime (indeed, some have become staunch supporters of sanctions against South Africa), they tend to put the East-West struggle well ahead of the racial struggle inside South Africa on their list of African issues; they warn, in fact, that a substantial Cuban presence in the region will strengthen the prospects that an allegedly communist-dominated African National Congress will impose a new, equally harsh tyranny on South Africa if it comes to power under black majority rule.

The moderate-centrist forces in U.S. politics have come to share many of the conservatives' propositions regarding the Cubans in Africa. Their attitude is perhaps best represented—even today—by some of the statements of the Carter administration on the subject in the late 1970s. Carter and his aides had a somewhat less cataclysmic view of the matter, but their remarks were not really any more subtle. President Carter, at a news conference in June 1978 said:

> We are doing the best we can to acquaint the world with the hazards and the consequences of increasing involvement of the Soviets and the Cubans in Africa. I think it's accurate to say that they take advantage of local disturbances and move with massive intrusions, both of military weapons, which contribute to further bloodshed among Africans themselves, and when they are permitted by the local government, they send in large quantities of troops.[5]

The Democrats were especially concerned at the time over the widespread perception (since shown to have been inaccurate) of Cuban involvement in the two consecutive invasions of the Shaba province of Zaire, in 1977 and 1978, by former Katangese gendarmes living in exile across the border in Angola. President Mobutu Sese Seko of Zaire, although widely recognized as a repressive ruler himself, has long enjoyed bipartisan U.S. support as a bulwark against communism in a strategically located and mineral-rich country, and so the specter of a Cuban-sponsored attack on him was very threatening indeed.

Moderate Democrats and liberal Republicans do not necessarily share the conservatives' reflexive reaction against the Cubans in Africa.

They might not object, for example, to Cuban contingents in Africa of a size modest enough to be portrayed as simple aid missions; they would still probably be regarded as doing "dirty work" for the Soviet Union, rather than being engaged in genuine development assistance, but would be understood and accepted as a natural part of the latest stage in the Cold War. The Cuban force in Angola, however—generally estimated in the United States to be between 25,000 and 35,000—causes serious domestic political problems for the moderates, who feel they dare not run the risk of being considered "soft on communism."

For the mainstream political "left" in the United States,[6] Cuba's presence in Africa has also become a problem. Cuba's contingent in Angola is regarded by many liberal activists as a distraction from the more important issues of Namibian independence and progress toward the dismantling of apartheid in South Africa; removal of the Cuban troops there is seen as the subject of an insidious linkage, available to the South Africans and the Reagan administration as a bargaining chip. On the Horn of Africa, the Cuban role looked very cynical and mischievous indeed. Hard as it was to justify the decades of U.S. support for the cruel and feudal regime of Haile Selassie, it is not easy to understand Cuban aid to Mengistu—a man who not only conducted a bloody purge of nearly all of his country's intellectuals, leaving many of those who did not have time to escape the country lying dead on the streets of Addis Ababa, but also cynically used Ethiopia's tragic famine to achieve some of his domestic political goals.

Even while recognizing that there are often legitimate distinctions between the Soviet and Cuban records in Africa—and that some Cubans, especially teachers and medical personnel, have done a great deal to promote the well-being of needy Africans—liberal Democrats have a hard time making this point with so many powerful forces arrayed against them. The apparent unwillingness of Cuban officials to take U.S. public opinion into account on this and other issues adds to the impression that one of Havana's real purposes in Africa is precisely to irritate and embarrass the United States. This in turn makes it more difficult for those who genuinely believe in the improvement of U.S.-Cuban relations, to the benefit of both sides—those who do not see any particular political benefit from Cuba-bashing—to make their voices heard in the policy debate. Politicians who urge that a dialogue with Cuba be returned to a place of priority on the U.S. foreign policy agenda are now frequently dismissed as naive.

Thus, the presence of a substantial Cuban expeditionary force on the African continent is a problem at all points on the U.S. political spectrum. To deal with this problem effectively will take imagination, patience, and compromise on both sides.

Any effort to break the deadlock on this issue must presuppose that both sides truly want to do so. It must be recognized, however, that in the most cynical sense, the conflict over the Cuban role in Africa serves certain ongoing political needs in both Washington and Havana. So long as the large contingent of Cubans remains in Angola, conservatives in the United States are able to blame them for much of the instability in southern Africa—and to get more of what they want, not only for Savimbi's UNITA, but also for the *contras* in Nicaragua, by raising the specter of "Cuban aggression" and interventionism. At the same time, for hard-liners in the Cuban regime who see anti-U.S. sentiment as the only durable, valid basis for Cuban foreign policy, the presence in Angola is a relatively inexpensive way to achieve dramatic results.[7] At the very least, it is a means for keeping the United States on edge. And in terms of its reputation and prestige in the Third World, Cuba gains a great deal from its support for the MPLA in Angola and its involvement at the margin of the South African conflict. Indeed, at the first session of the 3rd Cuban Communist Party Congress in Havana, in January 1985, Castro even seemed to suggest that Cuban forces might be in Angola not merely until the UNITA challenge was neutralized, but until apartheid was dismantled. Whether this was simply a trial balloon, or Castro had some other purpose in putting it forward, it was not adopted as Cuba's official position. By 1987, senior Cuban officials were insisting that all Castro had meant to say was that the front line African states could not feel secure as long as apartheid existed In South Africa. They emphasized, however, that the end of apartheid was *not* a precondition for the withdrawal of Cuban troops from Angola; rather, that would be contingent upon Namibian independence and the neutralization of the South African security threat to Angola.[8] In effect, then, Cuba's position, if it had ever changed, now closely parallels what it was in the early 1980s, when Castro was ready to discuss a phased withdrawal of Cuban troops from Angola provided South African troops simultaneously left Namibia (thus, in a sense, accepting U.S. ideas of "linkage" of the two problems). This illustrates the fact that some common ground does exist between the two positions.

Further, there are compelling reasons why U.S.-Cuban disagreements over Africa ought to be addressed. Those on both sides who have engaged in various sets of negotiations aimed at some level of rapprochement between Washington and Havana realize that even if some of the thorniest other issues—such as immigration, Cuban payment of compensation for nationalized U.S. properties, the lifting of the U.S. embargo, etc.—were to be resolved, the question of the Cuban role in Central America and Africa would still have to be raised by the U.S. side. If Cuba genuinely seeks some kind of opening in its relations with the United States, it will have to be willing to address disagreements in both areas—not in the sense of conceding the U.S. positions and demands, but rather of finding middle ground acceptable to all sides.

The United States, of course, would have to use a more imaginative approach than has been seen in recent years from either Republican or Democratic administrations. Both in the late 1970s, when Castro offered to cooperate with the United States and straighten out misunderstandings over the "Shaba II" incident in Zaire, and in the 1980s, when he offered a formula for phased withdrawal from Angola, U.S. officials rebuffed his overtures and preferred to remain on the attack. In the case of the Shaba crisis, the Carter administration simply called him a liar, on the basis of what many people knew was flimsy intelligence information tying Cuba to the invaders.[9]

Cuba has already shown itself to be immensely pragmatic in Africa. After the Shaba incidents, it helped bring about a degree of improved relations between Angola and Zaire (not exactly a revolutionary socialist state). It urged the South West Africa People's Organization (SWAPO) to accept the Western proposals for a settlement in Namibia at one point, and it supported the Lancaster House agreement of 1979 leading to independence for Zimbabwe, where it has ever since maintained a low profile.[10] Indeed, except for its continuing presence in Angola, Cuba has seemingly made few efforts to influence governments or events in the region; it has avoided provoking South Africa by staying out of Mozambique, where its expertise certainly might have been helpful in fighting the South African-backed guerrillas attempting to overthrow the Frelimo government led by the late Samora Machel.

If the United States were wise, it would attempt to invite Cuba back into the negotiating process in southern Africa, testing the sincerity of Angola and Cuba about wanting to cut back on the number of Cuban troops (in exchange for a meaningful South African withdrawal from southern Angola and some improvement in the situation in Namibia). If it is true, as some have reported, that unrest has grown inside Cuba over soldiers' deaths and injuries in Angola, then U.S. and Cuban interests may not be so far apart as is generally supposed.

Improbable as it seems, given the record of the past twenty-five years, Cuba and the United States might also find other congruent goals in southern Africa. For example, both would have a great deal to offer the Southern Africa Development Coordination Conference (SADCC), a regional organization seeking to reduce the dependence of neighboring countries on South Africa. Certainly any increased capacity of SADCC countries to stand on their own would make economic sanctions and other policies implying pressure on South Africa more effective.

Indeed, Cuban and U.S. ideas for South Africa's post-apartheid future need not be poles apart, and the prospect of U.S.-Cuban co-operation in southern Africa is a concept that would necessarily command great respect in Pretoria. As the United States government, under the influence of sanctions insisted upon by congress and a growing tide of withdrawals from South Africa by U.S. corporations, distances itself further from the apartheid regime, Washington and Havana might well find themselves agreeing on policy in the region to an extent that almost embarrasses them both. Certainly it is in the long-range interests of both countries that some progress be made toward a negotiated settlement in South Africa without a full-blown civil war, and that Angola be able to achieve some degree of stability without the presence of foreign troops.

The Angolan government advanced a plan, in November 1984, that provided for mutual and phased withdrawal of South Africans and Cubans from Angola and Namibia; if the United States were to look again at this plan, which had Cuban support, it might well find that it could form the basis for a new round of multilateral negotiations. One step that might be required, of course, would be a U.S. pledge to end support for Savimbi—if not a reinstatement of the Clark amendment (which is widely disliked in some quarters as an improperly specific constraint on the president's capacity to conduct foreign policy), then at least a declaration of a new official policy binding on the overt and covert agents of the United States—in order to give the MPLA govern-ment in Luanda greater confidence in its safety. As South Africa begins to find it more necessary to concentrate its full energies on its grave internal problems, this may well provide another opening for the solution of the Namibian problem in terms of U.N. Security Council Resolution 435. For the United States and Cuba to become, in effect, cosponsors of such a solution would be a dramatic development, welcome to many.

In fact, Africa may be just where Cuba and the United States can begin their long-delayed rapprochement. Successes there might lead in the long run to surprising and desirable developments elsewhere—a lesser Cuban reliance on the Soviet Union in the foreign policy field, a greater U.S. sense of security in Central America and the Caribbean, and a general relaxation of tensions between two countries that have so many intrinsic reasons for wanting to get along better.

Notes

1. See Smith, Wayne S. "Cuba, the U.S. and Africa." In *The Closest of Enemies*. (New York: W.W. Norton, 1987), p.128, and LeoGrande, William M. *Cuba's Policy in Africa, 1959–1980*. Berkeley, California: Policy Papers in International Affairs, Institute of International Studies, University of California, no.13, p.9.

2. LeoGrande, *Cuba's Policy in Africa*, pp.2 and 21.

3. LeoGrande, *Cuba's Policy in Africa*, pp.35–42.

4. U.S. Department of State Bulletin, Washington, D.C., February 1983, pp.73 and 76.

5. U.S. Department of State Bulletin, Washington, D.C., August 1978, p.6.

6. The U.S. "left" is defined here as the liberal wing of the Democratic Party. Although there still exist some socialist and Marxist activists in the United States who would meet the classical European definition of the "left," they are few in number and have little practical political influence.

7. It is generally assumed that Angola reimburses Cuba for much of the assistance it provides. See, for example, David Lamb, *Los Angeles Times*, May 21, 1980, Section I, p.17.

8. As stated by José Viera, Cuba's senior Vice Minister of Foreign Relations to a group of Americans on October 30, 1987.

9. See Smith, "Cuba, the U.S. and Africa," pp.198–9.

10. Ibid., pp.199–200.

3.2　Cuban Policy Toward Africa _____

Armando Entralgo Gonzalez
_____ David Gonzalez Lopéz

The general principles on which Cuba's policy toward Africa is based are clearly and systematically outlined in the official documents of the Cuban Revolution. But because the application of that policy has been perceived by successive U.S. administrations as contrary to the interests of the United States and its allies, a good number of the Western media, and not a few of the supposedly scientific centers which respond to those same interests, have tended to distort the objectives of Cuba's policy, dramatizing its impact and misrepresenting the essence of its actions. However, even a quick review of Cuban actions over the past twenty-five years confirms the faithfulness of policy to well-established principles.

Latin America and Africa came into contact as a result of the capitalist system's historic worldwide expansion. A three-way system of trade linked the societies of the two continents on all levels, and just as this *world wide economy* made them part of a dependent *periphery*, it also determined the role each would play in accumulating capital for those who ran the system. The presence of men of African ancestry and of Afro-American cultures in our lands, and thus the structural characteristics of the Caribbean, had their origins in the dynamic expansion of capitalism. The partition outlined in the 1885 Act of Berlin solved the needs of capitalist Europe for the period during which Spanish colonialism was being forced to retreat from its American colonies. Cuba is a good example of what would gradually happen in Latin America throughout the twentieth century. Cuba gained its independence in 1902, but remained economically and politically dependent on Europe, bringing to mind the case of many young African nations that proclaimed their independence in the 1960s.

47

Before 1959, in Cuba, as in other dependent Latin countries with significant black populations, bourgeois regimes that were modeled along European and U.S. lines instituted patterns of racial discrimination which tended to limit interest in Africa (except for a handful of people who were able to transcend the limitations of the era) to the superficial study of local peoples of African origin whose cultural manifestations were relegated to the world of folklore. And when, after World War II, the anti-colonial movements in Africa began their struggle against the colonial order, little information on those events reached Latin America; and what did was often distorted by the Western media, which still monopolized the distribution of information.

Cuba's limited diplomatic and consular relations with Africa (Ethiopia, Liberia and Nasser's Egypt) before 1959, were expanded after the triumph of the Revolution. In part, this was because of the wave of independence that swept over the Sub-Sahara in 1960, but it also stemmed from the changes in Cuban policy after 1959, and in the principles which sustained that policy. The Cuban Revolution naturally found ready acceptance on a continent which recently had been freed of colonial occupation and which was still victimized by the consequences of that experience.

What are these principles on which Cuban policy has been based since 1959? They are summarized below:

1. *Cuba denounces colonialism and supports wars of national liberation against colonialism.* Cuban representatives in the United Nations have articulated that view since 1959. Cuba gave more concrete form to the principle by offering full support to Algeria's quest for independence. Cuba also consistently condemned Portuguese colonialism, and indicated its unequivocal support for the liberation movements in the Portuguese territories.

2. *Cuba denounces South Africa's system of apartheid, or institutionalized racism, as well as that country's colonial presence in Namibia.* Cuba was also critical of the racism of the Rhodesian regime. It has from the beginning supported the ANC's battles in South Africa, South West Africa People's Organization in Namibia, and those of the nationalist organizations in Zimbabwe.

3. *Cuba denounces the capitalist superpowers' neocolonialist policies in Africa.* Cuba demonstrated its commitment to this principle by supporting the cause of Patrice Lumumba and the countries of the so-called Casablanca Group. From 1960 to 1963, that group represented the most committed effort in Africa's battle for true decolonization (in the economic, social, political, and cultural spheres), and for a policy of positive non-alignment in international relations.

4. *Cuba supports the cause of anti-imperialist unity among the*

African states. The unity movement culminated in 1963, with the formation of the Organization of African Unity. The OAU's principle goal was—and is—to eradicate from Africa the last bastions of racism, colonialism, and neo-colonialist meddling. Cuba supports the OAU, although some of its members (especially when the organization was first formed) have been extremely dependent upon foreign capitalist powers. Cuba especially supports, and respects for being true to the struggle, those countries that have chosen a non-capitalist path to development.

5. *Cuba has established diplomatic and cooperative relations with the various members of the OAU, regardless of their political systems.* These relationships are based on mutual respect for the principles of sovereignty, territorial integrity, and non-interference in internal affairs. The relations established with the governments of the Casablanca Group, and later with the Congo (Brazzaville) and Tanzania, were broadened, toward the end of the 1960s and the beginning of the 1970s, to include diplomatic ties and cooperation with a large number of countries that were active in both the OAU and in the Non-Aligned Movement and which were struggling to establish independent foreign policies, defend world peace, encourage a New International Economic Order, solve conflicts through negotiations, and enhance respect for the right of all peoples to choose the system under which they wish to live.

Based on these principles, and in spite of a lack of resources that would have allowed a large volume of trade or financial support for large-scale projects, the Cuban Revolution developed an intense program of assistance to Africa. The military aid that Cuba sent to Africa in response to requests from countries faced with attacks from abroad (which is allowed under Article 51 of the U.N. Charter) has, since 1975, monopolized the attention of those who control the international media. Nonetheless, the non-military aid Cuba has provided to Africa has often been greater, both in the quantity of the aid itself and in the growing number of nations that receive it. The following is a summary of the elements of Cuba's non-military assistance to Africa:

1. *Aid has been chosen to impact on areas in which Cuba itself had the most rapid success, especially in the fields of health and education.* In 1963, Cuba sent its first group of health workers to Algeria. Since then, such technical assistance has expanded to other countries or revolutionary peoples with whose leaders Cuba has established relations. The areas in which Cuba provides services have also expanded: Cuban specialists provide on-site training in Africa, but many Africans also come to Cuba to study and learn new technical skills.

During the decade of the 1980s alone, more than 13,000 African students have studied in Cuba.

2. *Cuba provides aid without preconditions or striving for profit.* Cuba sent its first doctors to Africa at a time in which the exodus of the profession from Cuba was creating difficulties in her own efforts to expand health care. By sending doctors to Africa, despite such considerations, Cuba established a precedent that set the tone for all of her technical assistance efforts. For Cuba, the extension of foreign aid is not a matter of gaining economic benefits, or of sending superfluous personnel abroad. It is a matter of expressing in a practical fashion the principles of internationalism; it is a way of repaying the debt of solidarity for the assistance provided by others so that the Cuban Revolution might survive. Cuba does derive some indirect benefits, nonetheless—mostly in the professional and ideological preparation of its tens of thousands of internationalist technicians, who acquire valuable experience from their work, often under exceptionally difficult circumstances. Until 1977, Cuba provided all assistance free of charge. Beginning in 1978, however, it began charging certain high-income countries, mostly those that were producing oil at a time when market conditions were good. This new income permitted Cuba to diversify and expand its non-military aid. Nevertheless, the essential internationalist principles on which such aid had been based from the beginning, remained unchanged. Those African countries suffering under economic difficulties continued to receive assistance free, and others were subsequently exempted from having to pay when faced with adverse economic conditions.

3. *Cuba has responded and adapted to existing conditions in each country.* Occasionally, it has supplied aid in response to an urgent situation even before establishing formal diplomatic relations. Cuba has also demonstrated the extent to which it is willing to adapt the provision of its aid to the conditions and needs of the recipient countries. Cuban workers in Africa live an austere style of life, and in Cuba, African students on the Isle of Youth follow a course of study especially designed for them, in which they are taught the history and language of their respective countries.

4. *Warm local acceptance and agreement with the spirit of South-South cooperation.* The special nature of Cuba's foreign aid has made it very popular in Africa. Many Africans have called it a model for South-South cooperation.

In spite of Cuba's gradual, multifaceted expansion in the areas of politics, diplomacy and non-military assistance in its relations with Africa, attention in the West has focused almost exclusively on Cuba's military aid to the region.

Most currently, this military assistance has taken the form of training African troops, but it has occasionally led to small numbers of Cuban advisers on African soil. In exceptional circumstances, such as in Angola, it has also resulted in the sending of combat troops. The first time Cuba did so, in Algeria in 1963, the action elicited no great controversy. But similar aid to the friendly governments of Angola and Ethiopia generated much speculation in the Western press.

The nature of the links and commitment that bind Cuba and Angola was defined on November 11, 1975, when the Popular Movement for the Liberation of Angola (MPLA) requested and Cuba extended military assistance under critical circumstances. Since then, Cuba has made clear its military solidarity with the cause of the Angolan Revolution—solidarity which preceded the MPLA's request for military assistance in 1975, and which was cemented by the identification of the two allies with one another's common past of oppression, rebellion and heroism, and their sense of brotherhood in a present that consists of an irrevocable commitment to internationalism. The governments and peoples of Africa applauded both the amount and the nature of Cuba's assistance to Angola, which was perceived as a substantive manifestation of Cuba's traditional support for anti-colonialist movements, and as a defense of juridical principles accepted by the U.N. and endorsed by the OAU. Those principles establish the right to self-determination and to the preservation of national sovereignty.

Although there were differences between the Ethiopian and the Angolan situations, the case of Ethiopia showed that African governments—including governments that had not requested troops—were neither surprised nor concerned over the presence of Cuban troops on the African continent.

Somalia, despite its expansionist aspirations during the early years of Siad Barre's rule, was not judged as harshly as South Africa by other nations, whether African or not. Barre's regime stemmed from a military coup that had promised to give the people of Somalia a less gloomy future, and had been accepted into the OAU with general approval. Nevertheless, when the government of Somalia invaded Ethiopia, and that country requested military aid from Cuba, other African leaders voiced no objection to the introduction of Cuban troops. Somalia had perhaps violated the most sensitive principle adopted by the OAU during its constitutional congress: The inviolability of national borders. Were it not for this principle, there would be an unending series of territorial claims throughout the African continent.

The presence of Cuban troops in Angola and Ethiopia over the past ten years enables us to draw certain rather precise conclusions about the circumstances which led to their arrival and to their continued stay:

1. The request for military assistance followed a break in negotiations, a failure to compromise, or a failure to agree on the part of one of the parties, which then chose to try for a quick military victory through foreign intervention. Cuba has made repeated efforts to reach peaceful agreements in Africa, even when such settlements would have required concessions on the part of friendly forces. Those efforts have been ignored.

2. Cuba's positive responses to the aggrieved parties' requests for assistance were endorsed by other African governments, and accepted by the OAU itself as appropriate to the defense of the sovereignty and territorial integrity of the region in the face of external threat.

3. Cuba responds with troops only in situations in which there is a concrete threat of aggression from abroad. Its role does not transcend recognized international borders; it does not represent a threat beyond those borders.

4. Continued Cuban presence depends entirely on the sovereign will of the receiving government and in no way impedes the parties' efforts to negotiate an end to the conflict and an agreement to bring about a long-lasting peace that would make the Cuban presence unnecessary.

Cuba's role in southern Africa exemplifies the principles that govern its policy toward Africa, particularly in relation to its military presence in Angola. In the 1980s, the prospect of a just and lasting peace in the region may seem further away. If so, that is due mostly to the policy of so-called *constructive engagement* of the Reagan administration. U.S. policy, moreover, ties the independence of Namibia to the withdrawal of Cuban forces from Angola, openly aids the Angolan counter-revolution and supports the South African regime at a time when it is facing growing internal unrest and isolation from abroad.

There is one point on which Cuba's perceptions of the problems in the southern cone of Africa is directly in line with that of international public opinion, and in direct contradiction to the positions of the current U.S. administration: That is, that the cause of regional instability in southern Africa is the existence of apartheid in South Africa. Since the 1970s, South Africa's relatively immobile political superstructure has given way to a state of almost uninterrupted unrest, and to an ever-widening and politicized popular battle against apartheid. Faced with the need for expansion and growth of monopolistic capitalism, the oligarchy had to rethink its position. It took its economic frustrations to the political arena and began steadily increasing its demands on the Nationalist Party, which was undermined in the process. In 1977, the government of Premier Vorster launched the first version of a limited program to reform apartheid, but Vorster was destroyed by his inability to satisfy the contradictory demands of his traditional political constituency, the monopolistic interests of South Africa's capitalists, who were supported by foreign interests, and the popular forces who were increasing pressure on the government. The government of Pieter Botha, who succeeded Vorster, seemed convinced of the need for deeper reforms, but succeeded only in polarizing the situation between the forces on the right who consider the reforms to be "suicidal," and the forces that clamor for an end to apartheid.

The most frequent interpretation of the regional problem in southern Africa, according to the line of thought held by the international community, is that the system of apartheid corresponds historically to the colonial period, but that in southern Africa the system has survived longer than it did elsewhere on the continent. The changes that were resisted by Portuguese colonialism, Rhodesian racism, and South Africa and its allies, began in the second half of the 1970s and transformed the face of the region. The new events resulted in a coalition of states just to the north of South Africa which have black majority governments and which are united in seeking political and economic directions independent of South Africa—thus, the creation of the front-line states and the Southern Africa Development Coordination Conference. But the internal policy of apartheid requires a foreign policy that provides for expansion beyond South Africa's borders. Both are policies that depend on the threat of force, or the actual use of force. For that reason, there will be no peace in the region until the last vestige of apartheid is eliminated in South Africa.

In March 1984, in a joint declaration, Cuba and Angola stated that if South Africa were to withdraw unconditionally from the territory it occupied in southern Angola, allow Namibia to become independent, in accordance with U.N. Security Council Resolution 435, cease all threats and acts of aggression against Angola, and if all U.S. and South African assistance to UNITA's counter-revolutionary troops were suspended, then the governments of Angola and Cuba would begin, on their own initiative, the gradual withdrawal of Cuba's internationalist military contingent. Such a withdrawal would begin with the removal, over a three-year period, of twenty thousand Cuban soldiers now located along Parallel 13. These conditions established the basis for a negotiated, just, and honorable settlement to the conflict in southern Africa.

However, South Africa and its allies, first among them the Reagan administration, either refused to negotiate, or insisted they could negotiate only from positions of strength. This pitted them against the OAU and the rest of the international community, who were calling for negotiated solutions. In January 1986, following trilateral talks among Cuba, Angola, and the Soviet Union, a communiqué was issued which laid out the prerequisite conditions for the withdrawal of Cuban troops and the participation of the signatories in a political solution to the conflict in the southern cone of Africa.

The communiqué pointed to South Africa's direct attacks on Angola, including its support of UNITA, as proof of its "sinister intent to eliminate Angola's progressive regime and make of Angola a vassal state of the Republic of South Africa and the international capitalist order." The communiqué also called the U.S. proposal to aid UNITA an "act of open interference in the affairs of sovereign Angola."

A series of events confirmed, however, that neither Pretoria nor Washington were prepared to negotiate a just peace in the region. In May of 1986, when a mediation team from the Commonwealth countries was visiting the region, South Africa attacked Zimbabwe, Zambia, and Botswana. It re-imposed a state of emergency one month later. Meanwhile, the United States, with the Clark Amendment having been abrogated, again began supplying arms to the Angolan counter-revolutionary forces. Soon, however, pressure from the anti-apartheid movement in the United States became so intense that the U.S. Congress imposed sanctions against South Africa over a presidential veto. The administration then hastened to revise its policy. This revision led to such unprecedented events as the meeting between George Shultz and Oliver Tambo in January 1987 and the renewal of contacts between the United States and Angola, which paved the way for a round of talks in Luanda in July and September of that year.

Even so, in the months that followed, the prospects for settlement seemed to become more distant than ever. While Angola and her friends showed flexibility and goodwill in an effort to reduce regional tensions, U.S. policy showed symptoms of fatigue. *Constructive engagement* seemed to approach the limits of its capacity for adaptation, and, paralyzed by its own internal contradictions, U.S. diplomacy seemed utterly bereft of ideas and initiatives to resolve the problems of southern Africa. Some observers attributed this paralysis to the Reagan administration's focus on other foreign affairs issues, as the president entered the last year of his tenure. Still other observers said the administration was caught between anti-apartheid groups, who advocated a greater distancing from South Africa, and ultra-conservative groups, who wished to maintain the confrontational climate in U.S.-Africa relations that has existed for some six years now, particularly with respect to the front-line states. To add to the confusion, U.S. officials often made contradictory statements on U.S. policy toward Africa, perhaps suggesting that the search for new political formulas to fill the post-Reagan era has already begun.

That the United States has no clear and coherent policy toward southern Africa augurs poorly for progress toward a just and lasting settlement in southern Africa before 1989. It is necessary, however, to review the situation the next administration will inherit. In the last months of 1987, the South African military launched an attack deep into Angolan territory. For the first time, high officials in the apartheid government confirmed that the goal of the action was to prevent the defeat of the Angolan counter-revolution. In an unusual act that violated all norms of international law, the President of the South African Republic and several of his ministers publicized a visit to South African troops stationed on Angolan territory.

In the U.N. Security Council, the U.S. representative, contrary to usual custom, did not veto the international community's condemnation of the attack.

Without calculating the extent to which they were in concert with the interests of those sectors of power in the United States who are openly arming the Angolan counter-revolution, South Africa's recent actions complicate the critical situation in the region at the same time that they confirm the failure of the so-called *constructive engagement* policy in the only area in which it had some attraction for South Africa's neighbors—that is, that the United States might play the role of *mediator,* and in the process exert a strong moderating influence on the aggressive nature of the apartheid government. This is now revealed to have been illusory. The United States apparently intended to play no such mediating role.

U.S. insistence on defending the system of apartheid over the past eight years has led to the increasing isolation of U.S. policy and to its virtual bankruptcy. Cuba's position, in contrast, has received growing support, both in Africa and in the international community. The validity of Cuba's principles has been upheld, and they have led, not to intransigence, but on the contrary, to flexibility and the desire to negotiate. Many public opinion polls, including some in the United States, have reflected support for the spirit of the August 3, 1987, Angolan-Cuban communiqué, in which the two countries stated their intention to "arrive at a just and honorable agreement that would allow for the independence of Namibia and guarantee the security of Angola and peace for all the southern African nations." The Cuban government has demonstrated its willingness to make sacrifices in the interest of a just and lasting resolution to the complicated problems in the region. Such a settlement requires, and this coincides with the majority opinion of the world community, an end to apartheid, which makes of South Africa a dangerous focus of instability.

Nevertheless, Cuba has agreed with Angola's efforts to use political negotiations to bring about Namibia's independence and an end to racist attacks and to South African and U.S. support of UNITA's counter-revolutionary forces.

Angola believes that if these requirements are met, and an international agreement guarantees that the country would no longer be attacked by South Africa, then the withdrawal of Cuban troops could take place. That is to say, we could arrive at a true global solution for Southwestern Africa (Angola and Namibia), and the total withdrawal of Cuban troops.

The Cuban government has stated on numerous occasions that its troops would not remain in Angola one day longer than desired by Angola's legitimate government, which called for Cuban support when it was in mortal danger. This danger has been present, to some extent, for the last twelve years. In recent months, however, South African attacks have escalated, becoming more intense than they have been since the period between October 1975 and March 1976.

These escalating attacks have met heroic resistance from the Angolan armed forces. Cuba has, nonetheless, been obliged to provide military reinforcements to contain South African advances. Even under these circumstances, the governments of Luanda and Havana have shown themselves willing to negotiate, as shown by their participation in a recent round of talks with U.S. representatives that took place in the Angolan capital, January 28 and 29, 1988.

An editorial that appeared recently in the official daily *GRANMA* clarifies the issue:

WHAT WOULD BE THE ESSENCE

OF A NEGOTIATED RESOLUTION

TO THE PROBLEMS OF ANGOLA AND NAMIBIA

It has been only a week since the round of negotiations took place in Luanda between the joint Angolan-Cuban delegation, and the representatives of the U.S., during which advances were made in the search for a political solution.

In these recent rounds, Angola laid out the required conditions for a just and honorable agreement.

• An end to foreign intervention in her internal affairs, in the form of U.S. and South African support for UNITAS' counter-revolutionary forces. This has resulted in the destruction of the economy of the

country and in sowing terror and death in defenseless villages.
- Removal of the South African forces that systematically invade Angola along its extensive southern and southeastern border.
- Implement the terms of U.N. Security Council Resolution 435, which will bring an end to the illegal occupation of Namibia by Pretoria's troops, and grant liberty to the last colony on the continent which has fought for its people under the leadership of SWAPO for many years.
- Provide international guarantees that there will be no further attacks on Angola.

If an agreement is reached on the basis of these conditions, Angola and Cuba are prepared to execute a plan for the gradual withdrawal of Cuba's internationalist military contingent, repatriating all our soldiers. This clear, just and objective proposal is based on international law, the U.N. Charter and a number of U.N. Security Council resolutions. A solution of this nature would be viewed with satisfaction by all the peoples of Africa and the world.

The solution now depends fundamentally on the attitude adopted by the U.S. government, as mediator in these negotiations. Its role is particularly important in efforts to bring an end to outside interference in the internal affairs of Angola, and in the firmness applied in support of a political solution in which the U.S. has expressed itself to be seriously interested.

South Africa could not defy the whole world community if the U.S. joined in unanimously demanding the implementation of U.N. Resolution 435.

South Africa may well be risking a total disaster in its military adventures in Angola—a disaster which could mean the swan song for the odious regime of apartheid. South Africa would lose relatively less from concessions and negotiations, therefore, than from continued intransigence.

Although brief, the discussions in Luanda were serious and represented an important step forward.

U.S. authorities have publicly expressed their satisfaction with the results of those talks.

A solution within a relatively brief time is objectively possible.[1]

Note

1. *GRANMA* (Havana, Cuba) 24 (29): 1, 4 February 1988, p.1.

4
DISAGREEMENTS IN THE UNITED NATIONS

4.1   Cuba in the United Nations _____

_____ Carlos Ciaño Zanetti

International organizations, and in particular the United Nations, are oriented towards regulating international relations, contributing to the peaceful solution of disputes, promoting international cooperation, and achieving the solution of diverse political, economic, and social problems.

Cuba has been a member of the U.N. from the time of its foundation, and, since the triumph of the Revolution, has played a particularly active role.   It is also a member of the Group of 77, which is comprised of underdeveloped countries and is a member of the Latin American Group in the U.N.

For that reason, the stands that Cuba takes in international debate, in addition to being determined by its particular political and economic perceptions, are also determined by the agreements made within the groups to which it belongs.

Cuba's activity within the United Nations is based fundamentally upon the principles that guide its foreign policy. The need to struggle for world peace and socio-economic development, in addition to the need to denounce aggression and promote solidarity in order to withstand such aggression, have represented the driving force behind the activity of Cuba in the United Nations.

I will attempt to analyze the position and voting record of Cuba in the U.N., utilizing a theoretical framework that was prevalent in the United States during the 1970s. This theory stated that Cuba's voting record illustrated its position as a satellite of the USSR, given the similarity found in the voting records of the two countries.

From 1977 until 1982, I had the good fortune of living in the United States and working in the Cuban Mission to the United Nations.

This allowed me to see from the inside what went on there. At the same time, using my contacts within some sectors of the North American population, I witnessed the satellite theory's development and utilization. It is not mere chance, in my judgement, that the emergence of this theory coincided with the growing strength of conservatism in the United States.

It is well known by all that Cuba and the USSR share the same ideology and sustain similar political ideas, therefore their positions must coincide much of the time. But Cuba has its peculiarities; in particular, its geographic location in this hemisphere, and having as a close neighbor a main enemy, whose aggression is increasing instead of decreasing. One example of a consequence is that Cuba either votes against or abstains on the issue of the Tlatelolco Treaty (which aims to create a nuclear-free zone in Latin America). This is in stark contrast to the position taken by the Soviet Union, which enthusiastically supports the treaty. Cuba's different position results from the situation it faces: a hostile United States loaded with nuclear weapons, some of which are positioned in Latin America. The United States even maintains a naval base on Cuba's territory—a base at which nuclear-armed ships frequently call. Under these circumstances, Cuba cannot simply sign away her right to have any kind of arms she needs for her defense.

Another of Cuba's peculiarities is its character as a developing country. Because of this, Cuba votes differently from the USSR on a whole series of economic and budgetary issues, as well as on the Law of the Sea. Cuba's voting pattern on these issues coincides with that of the majority of countries in the Non-Aligned Movement, not with the USSR.

As a developing country, Cuba is often able to act as a bridge between the socialist countries and those of the Third World, explaining the needs of the latter to the former in such a way as to help them adjust their positions to the realities of our part of the world. Since the end of the 1970s, the international economic crisis has worsened, and the Group of 77, to which Cuba belongs, has stepped up its criticism of the unfair economic practices of the developed countries of the West and has demanded an economic reordering on an international scale. In view of this, the positions of the socialist countries have moved increasingly closer to those of the developing countries, until it can now be said that in some cases, such as the resolutions over the New International Economic Order, the Letter of the Economic Rights and Duties of Countries, and the International Strategy of Development, there is a near harmony of views. The United States and its allies, on the other hand, have adopted completely opposite positions—positions that put them at odds with the vast majority of Third World countries.

In other words, what happened in the United Nations during these years was not that Cuba changed its way of voting so as to adapt to that of the USSR—in fact, Cuba has not changed its voting pattern at all—what has happened is that there has been a much higher level of activity on the part of the countries in the Third World, with which the positions of the socialist countries coincided, and therefore there was a greater number of resolutions in which Cuba and the USSR voted together.

In continuation, we offer some statistics concerning the voting patterns of the countries in the 39th Meeting of the General Assembly of the United Nations in 1984, which we consider to be important in demonstrating our theses.

Percentage of Times that Various Countries Voted with Cuba

Algeria	93.87
Yugoslavia	93.87
Mexico	93.53
USSR	93.19
Argentina	91.83
India	90.81
Egypt	89.79
United States	17.68

Cuba coincided with 51 countries more than 90 percent of the time; and with 106 countries more than 80 percent of the time.

Percentage of Times that Various Countries Voted with the USSR

Cuba	93.19
Algeria	87.75
Yugoslavia	87.75
Mexico	87.41
Argentina	85.03
India	84.69
Egypt	83.67
United States	24.48

The USSR coincided with 83 countries more than 80 percent of the time; with 115 countries more than 70 percent of the time; and with 16 countries less than 50 percent of the time.

Percentage of Times that Various Countries Voted with the United States

Great Britain	74.48
Federal Republic of Germany	68.70
Ivory Coast*	34.35
USSR	24.48
Cuba	17.68

*The Third World country that voted most often with the U.S.

The United States coincided with a single country more than 70 percent of the time; with 16 countries more than 50 percent of the time; and with 142 countries less than 50 percent of the time.

Voting Patterns by Region:

Western Hemisphere:

- 5 countries coincided with Cuba more than 90 percent of the time and 24 countries more than 70 percent of the time.
- 24 countries coincided with the USSR more than 70 percent of the time.
- One country (Canada) coincided with the United States more than 35 percent of the time.

Africa:

- 21 countries coincided with Cuba more than 90 percent of the time and 43 countries more than 80 percent of the time.
- 33 countries coincided with the USSR more than 80 percent of the time.
- No countries coincided with the United States more than 35 percent of the time.

Asia:

- 15 countries coincided with Cuba more than 90 percent of the time and 32 countries more than 80 percent of the time.
- 5 countries coincided with the USSR more than 90 percent of the time and 25 countries more than 80 percent of the time.
- 3 countries coincided with the United States more than 30 percent of the time: Japan, Australia and New Zealand.

Western Europe:

- 12 countries coincided with Cuba more than 68 percent of the time.
- 9 countries coincided with the USSR more than 68 percent of the time.
- 7 countries coincided with the United States more than 68 percent of the time.

Of the 147 Resolutions that reached a vote in the 1984 General Assembly, the United States only voted in favor of 16.

From these statistics, one can draw various conclusions, but two are particularly apparent:

1. The voting records of Cuba and of the USSR coincide, yes, but because they coincide with those of the vast majority of the member countries.

2. The United States is virtually isolated—tragically so—in the United Nations.

In addition, I think that these figures and the arguments presented prove that those who attempt to show that Cuba is simply a satellite of the USSR have not examined the statistics, nor have they made the most basic of analyses. The thrust of this theory, which I consider ill-conceived and misleading, has not only found some general resonance in the United States, but also, even more lamentably, among some who ought to be better informed.

Finally, I would like to refer briefly to two issues on which Cuba's voting has been different from that of the countries of the Third World. I am referring to the cases of Afghanistan and Kampuchea, and particularly to the first, which is very often used to attempt to demonstrate the *satellitism* or dependency of Cuba in relation to the USSR.

If we analyze the positions that Cuba has maintained historically in the face of the problems related to the battle for internationalism and against imperialism, it is impossible to conceive of Cuba as voting in any other way on issues such as these, given the firm and principled positions that Cuba has always maintained. We cannot conceive of Cuba voting with the United States or adopting lukewarm positions before situations such as these.

Independently of anything else, independently of any other criterion that we might have had, independently of the fact that it would have been a handicap in terms of our activity in the Non-Aligned Movement at the very moment we were stepping into the presidency, I think that to have voted in any other way would have been a case of political opportunism, and opportunism has never been a characteristic of the foreign policy of Cuba.

To pretend that this voting record reflects anything other than the logical and traditional stance that Cuba has always maintained is simply to refuse to recognize the most elemental of the positions that Cuba has maintained consistently in the field of international relations, or to take part in the campaign orchestrated to harm the image of Cuba.

4.2 Comments on "Cuba in the United Nations" _____

_____ Charles William Maynes

The first part of this chapter, by Carlos Ciaño Zanetti, is an example of the decades-long dialogue-of-the-deaf between Cuba and the United States about international affairs in general and U.N. policy in particular. What he says about Cuba's U.N. policy is at the same time neither wrong nor relevant. The concerns he is trying to address are not the concerns of U.S. policymakers.

No serious U.S. analyst, for example, expects Cuba to have a voting pattern that diverges significantly from that of most of the communist states which are members of the United Nations. Nor do they expect Cuba's voting pattern to differ significantly from that of most members of the Non-Aligned Movement.

Most U.S. observers of the United Nations and of the Third World understand that the agenda of the United Nations centers on three issues—the Middle East, southern Africa, and the North-South dialogue—on which the U.S. position is in the minority. Consequently, any analysis of U.N. voting patterns will reveal that few countries vote a majority of the time with the United States.

If that is so, what then is the U.S. complaint about the Cuban role in the U.N.? There are three parts to the complaint: First, U.S. observers contend that Cuba often plays an unnecessarily provocative role in the U.N. on issues that are particularly sensitive to the United States. One example would be the infamous Zionism-Racism resolution, on which the Cuban delegation assumed a leadership role. Another complaint would be the issue of the political status of Puerto Rico, on which the Cuban position often seems to be that Puerto Ricans can choose any political status they wish as long as it is independence. U.S. policymakers, on these and other issues, see Cuba as a country that goes out of its way to make statements or to take actions hostile to U.S. interests. That the country responsible for these actions is also closely tied to the Soviet Union only makes matters worse.

Second, although U.S. policymakers understand that Cuba will regularly vote similarly to the Soviet Union, they look carefully at votes where it seems to them Cuba has a legitimate reason for deviating from the Soviet position because of Cuban interests in the Non-Aligned Movement. When such deviations almost never take place, the conclusion reached in Washington is that Cuba is not and never was a truly non-aligned country.

It is from this perspective that one must begin to analyze the U.S. reaction to the Cuban position on Afghanistan or on North-South issues. Because the Soviet Union subsidizes Cuba's economy to such an extraordinary extent, few U.S. analysts expected Cuba to oppose directly the Soviet invasion of Afghanistan, even though Cuba was then head of the Non-Aligned Movement and Afghanistan was a non-aligned country. But the case for a Cuban abstention was strong. By abstaining, Cuba could have both admonished and reassured the Soviet Union: its abstention could have informed Soviet leaders that there were limits to Cuban support if the Soviet Union acted imprudently. Yet an unwillingness to join the vast majority of non-aligned states in condemning the Soviet action could have demonstrated Cuban willingness to take Soviet interests into account. Cuba, however, almost alone among the non-aligned states, voted with the Soviet Union on this issue.

Occasionally, Cuba has made small adjustments in its policy that have attracted attention in Washington. In the late 1970s, Cuba did try to work out a U.N. formulation for resolving the question of Puerto Rico's status that might have attracted the support of both those in favor of the commonwealth status and of independence. But it abandoned this effort after only one year. Fidel Castro did gingerly raise the issue of greater Eastern European support for development efforts in the Third World, but this initiative was also quickly dropped.

The Third part of the U.S. complaint about Cuban policy in the United Nations, paradoxically, relates to areas that Cuban officials regularly underscore in their effort to prove that Cuba is not a Soviet puppet in its foreign policy: it may be true that Cuba takes an even more "principled stand" on some international issues than the Soviet Union, but such a revelation does not reassure Washington. Rather it confirms a view that as bad as the Soviet Union may be from the standpoint of U.S. interests, Cuba is only worse. Moreover, citing such policy differences between Cuba and the Soviet Union does not prove to the United States that Cuba has an independent foreign policy. Just as a cheerleader for another team is not seen as independent from that team but simply as fulfilling a different role, so is Cuba seen by many U.S. citizens as simply a cheerleader within the communist community of states for even more radical policies. What Cuba sees as signs of independence, the United States sees as the exaggerated efforts of a client-state to curry favor with its superpower patron. The exception would seem to be Cuba's position on the Non-Proliferation Treaty, where its fear of and hostility toward the United States is even greater than its dependence on the Soviet Union.

It should be noted that U.S. paranoia about Cuban actions and statements sometimes results in the United States singling Cuba out for attention and attack when its actions may differ little from those of others, including states close to the United States. But just as Cuba has grounds for its fear of the United States, so the United States has grounds for its paranoia about Cuba. Over the years, Cuban diplomats have gone out of their way to create difficulties for the United States in multilateral institutions. When they are only joining the crowd, U.S. diplomats may be excused for wondering whether Cuba is not again, but this time more deceptively, playing an unnecessarily provocative role.

Can this negative pattern be changed? Not immediately, because the overlay of history is too great. But if both sides began by making realistic assessments of what the other is capable of doing, and then attempted jointly to minimize friction and irritation on the few issues where some freedom of action seemed possible, over time a greater degree of trust and cooperation might develop.

Such an approach may in fact be the best way to strengthen the United Nations itself. In large part, the international body finds itself in its present, very weak, situation because member states forget that the purpose of membership is to identify areas where they can cooperate, not fight with one another. Is it too much to ask that occasionally Cuban and U.S. diplomats remember this point in conducting their nations' policies in the United Nations?

Part 2
BILATERAL PROBLEMS

ECONOMIC AND COMMERCIAL ISSUES

5.1 The Issue of Claims as Seen by the United States

_____ Kirby Jones

Any discussion of the resolution of claims between Cuba and the United States must first begin with the realization that this is not simply a bilateral question involving dollars and cents. Rather, it is but one part of a complex and emotional issue between the two countries that has been festering in limbo for more than twenty-five years.

There are political issues involved that go well beyond the simple question of dollars and cents, there are emotional issues resulting from the separation of personal lives, and there are the overall diplomatic and face-saving issues involved when big powers and little powers confront each other.

It is in this context that the particular issue of claims must be viewed.

A brief look at the background behind the claims issue is important to set the stage for any understanding of its future resolution.

In late 1959, Cuba stopped all dollar transfer payments to the U.K. and U.S. petroleum suppliers and allowed USSR crude oil to enter Cuba. U.S. firms refused to refine this oil and in retaliation, in August, 1960, Cuba nationalized these U.S. firms. A series of steps by both sides then followed which resulted in the United States cutting off the Cuban sugar quota and in the eventual U.S. blockade.

Cuba did offer a repayment plan for the nationalized companies: This involved a provision of compensation in 30-year bonds at 2 percent interest to become effective if the then prevailing U.S. sugar quota (then 3.2 million tons per year) as well as the U.S. price of sugar were both raised.

From the U.S. point of view, these actions by Cuba violated accepted standards of international law that required the payment of adequate, prompt, and effective compensation. In addition, according to the United States, Cuba's actions also violated Article 24 of Cuba's own Constitution which (1) guaranteed protection of property on a non-discriminatory basis; and (2) established juridical procedures for special cases involving expropriation, stating that property could only be expropriated for just cause involving a public utility or social unrest, and then only through prior indemnification of the owner in cash as determined by the courts.

But from the Cuban point of view these actions were indeed warranted based on three decrees: (1) Agrarian Reform Law of June 3, 1959; (2) Law of Nationalization of July 6, 1960; and (3) Law 890 of October 14, 1960.

In 1964, the U.S. Congress amended the International Claims Settlement Act to direct the Foreign Claims Settlement Commission to determine the amount and validity of all claims.

There can be no doubt that part of the problem with any settlement of this issue is what sets it apart from all other such situations involving claims—that being the sheer size and amount of the claims involved.

The total of U.S. claims against Cuba is more than three times the combined total of claims awarded in Yugoslavia, Poland, Bulgaria, Hungary, Romania, the Soviet Union, Czechoslovakia, and China. In looking at the nature of the claims, two aspects become clear: individuals with claims far outnumber companies (although it is the corporate voice that is almost always noticed on this issue) and most of the claims are small—again contrary to popular belief. A look at the numbers will bear this out.

The United States has certified claims totaling $1,799,548,568.69. Added to this are the additional $200 million of claims of the U.S. government itself. The total number of awarded claimants is 5,911, of which 898 are corporate and 5,013 are individual.

Of all claims, 66 percent are less than $10,000 and 87.9 percent are less than $50,000. In numbers alone, only 104 claims are more than one million dollars, while 4,341 are under $5,000.

The following two tables provide a capsule look at some of the numbers involved:

Type of Claimant	Number Filed	Number Awarded	Number Denied	Number Awarded
Corporate	1,146	898	248	$1,578,498,839.55
Individual	7,670	5,013	947	221,049,729.14
Total	8,816	5,911	1,195	$1,799,548,568.69

Ten Highest Certified Claims

Claimants:

1. Cuban Electric Co. (Boise Cascade)	$267.6 million
2. ITT	130.7
3. North American Sugar Industries (Borden)	109.0
4. Moa Bay Mining Co. (Freeport Minerals)	88.3
5. United Fruit Sugar Co. (United Brands)	85.1
6. West Indies Sugar Co.	84.9
7. American Sugar Co. (now AMSTAR)	81.0
8. Standard Oil (now EXXON)	71.6
9. Bangor Punta Corp.	53.4
10. Texaco	50.1

These tables show several factors: First, many of the corporate claimants will probably never conduct any future business with Cuba. This is particularly true with utilities, cement, and oil companies. Second, almost as many claims by dollar amount were rejected as were accepted—approximately $1.8 billion was accepted while $1.4 billion was rejected. Third, many claims filed in the United States were based on asset value while the same company had filed a different value in Cuba, for domestic tax purposes. Lone Star Cement, for example, filed a claim in the United States for $24.8 million, on assets which had a declared value in Cuba, for taxes, of only $1.6 million. This becomes important during any settlement, as both sides could be using different figures.

With this as a brief compilation of the numbers involved, how can all of this be settled? Some experiences with other countries may indicate possible solutions. Between 1917 and 1949, the Soviet Union, Yugoslavia, Poland, Romania, Bulgaria, and Hungary expropriated large amounts of foreign-owned property. The lump sum settlement agreements negotiated by the United States are summarized briefly as follows:

- *Soviet Union:* In November, 1933, the United States and the USSR agreed to settle certain claims by the assignment to the United States of assets due the Soviet government as the successor of prior agreements of Russia. Only 9.7 percent of U.S. claims were compensated under this arrangement and then only after twenty years of litigation.
- *Yugoslavia:* By an agreement in 1949, Yugoslavia agreed to create a fund of $17 million to resolve claims for nationalizations to that date. That yielded a compensation rate of 91 percent,

but at the same time, the United States agreed to release $40 million in blocked gold bullion in return for the $17 million cash payment. Claims were settled finally by a 1964 agreement which called for a payment by Yugoslavia over five years of a total of $3.5 million, resulting in the compensation of 36.1 percent of U.S. claims.

- *Bulgaria:* A 1963 agreement provided for a settlement payment of $35 million, of which $400,000 was paid by Bulgaria, and the rest was taken from Bulgarian assets in the United States. The United States received a return of 69.7 percent.

- *Romania:* In 1960, Romania agreed to pay $25 million in cash over six years in addition to the $22 million in blocked assets. This was a 37.8 percent recovery.

- *Hungary:* In 1973, Hungary agreed to pay $118.9 million over a twenty-year period plus $3.32 million in blocked assets. In this case, twenty-eight years elapsed from the time of claims accrual to eventual settlement.

- *Poland:* In 1960, Poland agreed to pay the United States $40 million over twenty years and the United States agreed to release blocks on Polish assets.

- *China:* In 1979, the PRC agreed to pay $80.5 million in full payment for all claims with an initial payment in October, 1979, and the balance in five annual payments of $10.1 million starting in 1980. This agreement provided for a compensation of 40.9 percent.

- *Czechoslovakia:* Claims still exist and the settlement negotiated by the U.S. government has been rejected by the Congress.

- *Democratic Republic of Germany:* No claims settlement.

In looking at these various experiences with other communist countries, no clear pattern nor single solution was applied in all cases; each country was different. One could, therefore, conclude that previous experiences will not apply to Cuba. Although this may be true with respect to the particular cases, there still are some overall lessons that can be applied to the Cuban case.

First, no claims were made before the normalization of relations. This is very important in the case of Cuba, as will be discussed later. Second, no payment was anywhere near 100 percent of the certified claim. Third, there was a substantial time lag involved in the final settlement.

Over the past years, although there have never been any real efforts actually to settle the issue, there have been both attempts to outline the conditions for settlement of the claims as well as efforts to prevent settlement.

The question of the claims and settlement is not simply an isolated, bilateral issue to be resolved by government negotiators. Rather, it has more to do with domestic U.S. political concerns than it does, or will do, with the two governments. Both governments have long, historical experience in resolving claims with other countries; there is no reason to believe that the same people cannot negotiate a solution in this case as well—even with the large dollar amount of these particular claims. Rather, what have been and are present in the case of Cuba are emotional and political issues carried by a body of individuals and companies which do not want a solution to this issue. Up to now, this outlook has coincided with that of the U.S. government.

This overtly manifested itself first in the late 1970s, with the actions of the Joint Corporate Committee on Cuban Claims which was formed under the leadership of representatives of Lone Star Industries, Bangor Punta, and others. This group of fifty-eight companies hired a prestigious Washington-based law firm and fought articulately and effectively to put forth a position which made it clear that the companies wanted something that had never been done before with any country—a resolution of the claims settlement *before* normalization.

This group testified before Congress and publicized its case with easy access to the media. Since there was no effective force on the other side, the impression was created that U.S. business in general agreed with their position.

At times, however, certain members of this committee acted out of both sides of their company. Amstar, for example, was a leading force opposing trade within the committee while at the same time its sugar traders were regularly meeting with Cuban officials in Europe trying to arrange deals through its subsidiary.

In addition, while these fifty-eight companies were lobbying against normalization, representatives of over 200 companies were traveling to Cuba to prepare for what they hoped would be an eventual chance to trade with Cuba. These 200 included many companies which had claims. None of these were able—or wanted—to negotiate their claims directly with Cuba. Many echoed the feelings expressed by the representative of International Harvester who told the Chicago Tribune upon returning from Cuba that "we figure the claims situation is a matter to be worked out between governments. We will look toward getting our money back by selling our product there."

These more than 200 companies, however, never were able to mount an effective lobbying effort in favor of normalization. This left a vacuum into which the fifty-eight companies against normalization were able to carry the day—at least in the public eye.

The simple catch 22 involved was, and remains, as follows: If, according to the fifty-eight companies, normalization should not proceed until claims are settled, then claims will never be settled at all since, without a process to normalize, the mechanics to negotiate a claims settlement can never develop.

One thing is absolutely clear—no claims have been paid to U.S. companies or individuals in over twenty-five years. At the same time, however, Cuba has settled its claims with other market economy countries. A continuation of the current policies can in no way be expected to change that negative condition. Without some motivation to settle claims, Cuba can be expected to do nothing. Cuba has already not only settled claims with others, but has stated on many occasions its willingness to enter into discussions to settle U.S. claims as well.

There is nothing special about the Cuban situation that would lead one to expect Cuba to be unique in recent history—that is, to settle claims before normalization begins to take place.

However—and this is important—if U.S. policymakers one day do take steps to normalize, but do it piecemeal and in public, such a process will only allow such groups as the fifty-eight to mount another counter-effort and thus possibly torpedo the very efforts the U.S. government might wish to mount. The United States should instead negotiate a package of agreements which includes a mechanism to settle claims all together and in the privacy of diplomatic channels. This is what President Nixon did with China to avert the pressures of the China lobby (and indeed, what Henry Kissinger did in July, 1974, to open up the first channels of communication with Cuba).

What about Cuban counter-claims? Cuba has stated that it too has claims against the United States. As a result of the Bay of Pigs, the blockade, and other actions, the Cubans maintain that their claims are more than the $1.8 billion certified in the United States.

Making counter-claims is not a new approach—Peru, for example, made counter-claims against the International Petroleum Company for "back taxes" when Peru nationalized that firm, and Chile argued that U.S. copper companies owed it money for "excess profits" when Allende nationalized the copper companies.

This should be taken as Cuba's opening bargaining position—just as they must take the U.S. demand for 100 cents on the dollar as its opening hand. There are no actual precedents that indicate that Cuba would not enter into a serious set of meetings to settle this issue—especially if there were motivation to do so and if there were something to lose if it did not.

The question, then, from the U.S. point of view is how it—one day—will be able to accomplish its foreign policy goals and normalize relations with Cuba without letting the anti-forces impede that process. Keep in mind one thing—any U.S. president must be able to announce a settlement of the claims issue, or at the least a plan to settle the claims, if he is to be able to make normalization with Cuba politically possible. On the other side, Cuba would have to be uncharacteristically naive not to understand this point as well.

To the fifty-eight companies who are against normalization, it can only be said that such a step is their only chance to receive any money, despite the fact that they do not understand or take this position now.

As negotiations might begin, a number of assumptions can be made with regard to any settlement: Cuba will not pay any money to companies or firms directly; any agreement will be between the two governments; the U.S. government will have to decide how to allocate whatever funds might be available; Cuba will not pay 100 cents on the dollar, whether it is the $1.8 billion claimed or the many more billions when the 6 percent interest is included; Cuba would like to minimize the amount of hard currency it will have to expend; U.S. firms and individuals will want as much cash as possible.

How can this be accomplished?

There have been a number of ideas, resolutions, and proposals that have been developed over the years—some of them imaginative, none of them productive or implemented. Some have come from the U.S. Congress and some have come from the private sector. Without discussing all of the proposals that any one organization or individual have put forth, most are similar to some of the following:

- In 1979, Senate Joint Resolution 87 and House Joint Resolution 355 expressed the sense of the Congress to guide the President. It set payment in full plus interest as a pre-condition for negotiation with the Cuban government. The U.S. government took strong exception to this possible resolution saying that such a policy would only tie the hands of any negotiators while at the same time stating that the trade embargo would not be lifted until a formula for settling claims had been agreed.
- Tax credits could be issued in the amount of the claims. But certified claims are far in excess of tax losses, and to those Corporations which have not been profitable since expropriation, there would be no tax benefit anyway. Tax credits would not serve the small individual claimant. Some companies have rejected this plan since they claim they have lost not only the value of assets, but income from business as

well.

- Royalties on Cuban products, including nickel, copper, iron ore, petroleum, and sugar, could be paid over a long period of time in amounts to be negotiated. Some type of security issued with evidence of debt with the administration of the plan could be carried out by an international agency such as the International Monetary Fund or the U.N. But Cuba is not a member of the IMF, and it is likely the IMF would not want to carry out the job anyway.

Given the increasing utilization of new financial instruments that are in practice today, and given the acceptability of these schemes, some new alternatives that might have seemed unworkable yesterday may now not only be possible, but even seem commonplace. If U.S. banks can swap debt for U.S. government-backed Mexican securities, if companies can swap debts with each other, if debts can be turned into equity, if transfers of money are implemented with the push of an electronic button, then imaginative plans might be possible in the case of Cuban claims as well. One such plan or swap might work this way:

- The United States and Cuba negotiate a dollar amount to settle the claims issue;
- Cuba issues what would be the equivalent of certificates of obligation in these amounts;
- The U.S. government allocates these certificates to the claimants according to its own plan.
- At the same time, Cuba amends its investment regulations so that these certificates have value in Cuba against investments or trade;
- The U.S. recipients sell their certificates, as they would any debt security, to companies or firms—foreign or domestic—which may be then or would be in the future doing business with Cuba (individuals or corporations who hold these certificates would sell them through already existing Wall Street firms);
- The certificates would be sold at a discount price. A holder of a $10,000 certificate, for example, would sell it to a company for $5,000 in cash. This company could then redeem the certificate in Cuba for the face value of $10,000 in tax or business concessions;

For the corporation claimants in the United States, which now hold an asset with a book value equal to the certified claim but a real value in the marketplace of zero, this plan represents a chance to receive at least some money.

For Cuba, which now holds a liability that others expect it to pay with hard currency, this represents the chance to exchange that foreign hard currency liability for a local currency obligation.

For the purchaser of these certificates from the United States claimant, they receive full value at a discount price.

This has never been tried before in any other claims situation—but then again, the world has not really faced such a claims issue involving the emotions or the dollar amounts as this one.

The settlement of any and all claims between the United States and Cuba simply depends on a desire to do so. Both sides have been through the process before, both sides have indicated a willingness to deal with the issue, and both sides certainly do not and would not want this relatively simple issue to be the one to derail any more substantial effort to reach a bilateral diplomatic understanding.

To be sure, there are those who do not want a resolution of this issue—either because of the financial interests involved or because of some emotional tie to the past. Neither of these positions can be allowed to upset U.S. foreign policy interests. To do so would be shortsighted and counterproductive.

At the same time, from the Cuban point of view, an equal degree of flexibility and reality is necessary, and I expect will be forthcoming at the right time. In other situations, and with other similar issues, Cuba has demonstrated diplomatic sensitivity and dependability. There is no reason to expect Cuba not to act in the same serious and forthcoming manner to end the stalemate between the two countries.

The claims issue should not be a major stumbling block to such negotiations and once the day arrives when there is a normal state of relations between Cuba and the United States, the claims issue will be remembered as are other past claims issues—that is, as a footnote to larger and more historically important matters.

5.2   The U.S. Trade Embargo _____

Lilia Ferro-Clerico
Wayne S. Smith

The argument as to whether imposition of the U.S. trade embargo reflected latent hostility to the Cuban Revolution, or rather, was provoked by unfair Cuban confiscatory policies, is like the argument over the chicken and the egg: There is no definitive answer; there is only subjective postulation.

Most Cuban observers insist that it was an almost Pavlovian U.S. rejection of Cuba's Agrarian Reform Law, in the summer of 1959, which touched off the train of events leading to the trade embargo.   U.S. observers, on the other hand, note that the United States did *not* reject the agrarian reform. Quite the contrary. The U.S. diplomatic note of June 12, 1959, which responded to the reform law, specifically acknowledged Cuba's full right to implement such a reform; it objected only to the terms of compensation. And even in that regard, there was no flat rejection.   Rather, it seemed to be the intention of the United States to continue efforts to secure better terms. Certainly no economic reprisals were undertaken or even suggested at that time.

Whatever the role played by the agrarian reform, an event that more directly triggered the embargo was the visit to Cuba of Soviet Deputy Prime Minister Anastas Mikoyan in February of 1960. At the conclusion of that visit, he and Prime Minister Fidel Castro signed a trade agreement under which the Soviet Union committed itself to purchase 5 million tons of sugar over a five-year period; to supply Cuba with crude oil and petroleum products, as well as with wheat, iron, fertilizers, and machinery; and to provide Cuba with a $100 million credit at 2.5 percent interest.[1] This agreement helped to convince many in the United States that the die was cast, that is, that Castro had decided to ally himself with the Soviet Union and to integrate Cuba into the socialist bloc's economic system.

In early June of 1960, just before the first Soviet oil arrived in Cuba, the foreign oil companies there—Shell, Esso, and Texaco—informed the Cuban government that they would not refine it. Castro warned that if they did not, they would have to accept the consequences. The companies nonetheless refused, claiming that not to do so would interfere with their principles of managerial control.[2] In fact, it is now known that the U.S. government had encouraged them not to refine the Soviet oil.

The consequences Castro had warned of came quickly. On June 29, Cuba nationalized the Texaco refinery, and on July 1, those of Esso and Shell. The U.S. Congress then responded to these seizures by passing, on July 3, the Sugar Act, which authorized the President to eliminate Cuba's sugar quota. On July 5 it was Cuba's turn again. It retaliated for the Sugar Act by nationalizing all U.S. businesses and commercial property in Cuba.

The following day, on July 6, President Eisenhower cancelled the 700,000 tons of sugar remaining in Cuba's 1960 quota. In announcing this measure, Eisenhower stated that "this action amounts to economic sanctions against Cuba. Now we must look to other moves—economic, diplomatic and strategic."[3]

The Soviet Union immediately stepped in to announce that it would buy the 700,000 tons of sugar cut by the United States.

When the Urban Reform Law went into effect in October of 1960, thus leading to another round of nationalizations, this time of rental properties owned by Americans, the Eisenhower administration declared a partial embargo to exist on trade with Cuba. It has been argued, however, that this step may have been due more to U.S. internal political pressures than to the new nationalizations.[4] In effect, Cuba had by then become an issue in the presidential electoral campaign. The Eisenhower administration felt that it could not afford to be charged with being soft on Castroism, so the embargo was imposed, as Richard Nixon explained, as an "all-out quarantine—economically, politically and diplomatically—of the Castro regime."[5]

John F. Kennedy, the Democratic candidate, dismissed the newly declared quarantine as useless, noting that it was a unilateral measure that did not have the support of the European countries, or even of the other Latin American states. The Eisenhower administration had counted on the OAS to support U.S. trade pressures against Cuba, but that had not happened. A key statement issued by the OAS Meeting of Foreign Ministers in August of 1960, for example, did not even mention Cuba, let alone call for economic sanctions.[6]

Upon his inauguration as President, in January of 1961, John F. Kennedy set out to gain the support of the OAS, which he saw as prerequisite to an effective embargo. He succeeded. At the Eighth Meeting of OAS Foreign Ministers, held a year later in January of 1962 at Punta del Este, Uruguay, Cuba was excluded from the Inter-American system and an arms embargo was imposed.[7] Having thus gotten the OAS behind him, on February 7, 1962, Kennedy proceeded to broaden the partial trade restrictions imposed by Eisenhower to a ban on all trade with Cuba, except for the non-subsidized sale of foods and medicines.[8] This single exception was removed in 1964, at the same time that all member nations of the OAS were called upon to prohibit trade with Cuba. From that time forward, the ban on U.S. trade with Cuba has been well nigh complete—even though, in 1975, the OAS itself lifted the multilateral sanctions imposed in 1962 and 1964, thus leaving it up to each member state as to whether it wished to have diplomatic, trade, and other relations with Havana.

U.S. Objectives

The United States had several objectives in moving toward and finally implementing a full trade embargo. First, beginning in March of 1960, the United States began to work for the downfall of the Castro regime. In effect, President Eisenhower's policy of non-intervention, contained in his proclamation of January 26, 1960, was set aside, and "[the] new American policy—not announced as such but implicit in the actions of the United States government—was one of overthrowing Castro by all the means available to the U.S. short of the open employment of American Armed Forces in Cuba."[9] By causing extreme economic hardship to the Cuban people, the embargo was intended to foster enough dissent to lead eventually to the downfall of the new regime.

Second, even should it fail to topple the regime, the embargo was deemed worthwhile in that it would make the Soviet-Cuban relationship as costly as possible to both. At best, it was reasoned, this might lead one, or both, to decide the price was too high, and, consequently, to reduce, or even to sever, those newly formed ties. At the very least, it would make it painful to them to continue the relationship—and thus have, if nothing else, a punishing effect.

Third, the embargo was intended to have a two-fold demonstration effect. Imposed partly in retaliation for the nationalization of U.S. properties, it was intended to serve as a deterrent to other countries that might contemplate such nationalizations, that is, to thus protect the interests of U.S. property owners. At the same time, by contributing to the failure of the economic model, it would make the revolutionary experience less attractive to other countries that might think of following Cuba's example.

As set forth in the announcement of the embargo, a final objective was to deprive the Cuban government of hard currency earnings which the United States believed might be used, at least in part, to finance Cuban "export of revolution."

Actual Effects of the Embargo

Twenty-five years later, it can be seen that the results of the embargo were, at best, mixed, and that it has paid steadily diminishing dividends. Indeed, at this point, one can argue that the embargo impedes more than it advances the achievement of U.S. objectives.

Obviously, the embargo did *not* lead to the fall of the Castro regime. On the contrary, rather than causing increasing dissent, it was used by the Castro government as a rallying point, allowing the Cubans to blame their hardships and economic difficulties on the United States and thus to fuel anti-U.S. sentiment. Rather than encouraging internal opposition to the government, it may actually have discouraged it. That argument aside, the fact is that the revolutionary government today is firmly in place and in a process of institutionalization. There should be no further illusions that maintaining the embargo will appreciably affect the stability or legitimacy of that government.

Initially, the embargo did cause extreme hardship to the Cuban economy. It is no exaggeration to say that Cuba's entire economy was tightly tied to the United States. Virtually every piece of machinery, from industrial plants to refrigerators, was U.S.-made.[10] Some 60 percent of Cuba's trade was with the United States. Basic foodstuffs, such as rice, were imported from the United States. As this source was abruptly closed, and Cuba could not even obtain spare parts for its U.S. machine-based economy, it faced the massive and costly task of converting at forced draft to Soviet-supplied equipment and industrial products and to a radically new economic system. The embargo did, then, for a time, definitely raise the cost to both the Soviets and the Cubans.

But more than twenty-five years have now passed. Cuba has long since made the transition to an economy closely integrated with those of the socialist countries. Almost all the old U.S. machinery has now been replaced with Soviet, East German, and Czech equipment. Some U.S. officials may argue that the embargo continues to impose a significant hardship on Cuba,[11] but most independent observers doubt its continued efficacy. Jorge Perez Lopez, a noted economist in the United States, for example, places the average annual growth rate of the Cuban economy at 7.3 percent for the period 1981 to 1985.[12] Such a growth rate, which is higher than that experienced by the other Latin American countries, would indicate that the embargo has very little residual impact. It is an inconvenience, nothing more.

Further, if one initial objective in "raising the cost" was to discourage the consolidation of the Soviet-Cuban tie, maintaining the embargo a quarter of a century later has exactly the opposite effect: it leaves Cuba with little alternative but to continue to rely heavily on the Moscow connection. This is not to suggest that were it not for the embargo, Cuba would sever its economic ties with the socialist bloc. Of course not. But it is virtually an inscribed law of politics that any country that is as dependent upon another as Cuba is on the Soviet Union will wish to reduce that dependency. By offering a viable alternative, the United States could *reduce* Cuban-Soviet economic ties—in time, perhaps significantly.

Nor did the embargo deter Cuban support for national liberation movements in Latin America. In fact, one could more persuasively argue that it further stoked the fires by increasing Cuba's sense of isolation. The most intense period of Cuban support for revolution began just *after* the imposition of the embargo and continued during the years of its most painful impact, 1963 to 1968. Cuba's pursuit of this aggressive line began to taper off in 1968, and by 1982, at a time when (as stated previously) the embargo had little remaining effect, Cuban theorists had come around to saying there were only two countries in the hemisphere in which conditions for revolution existed, and even in those countries, El Salvador and Guatemala, Cuban support for revolutionary movements had become increasingly tenuous and Cuba more ready to discuss compromise solutions with the United States (see Chapter 2 on Central America).

In sum, one can make a better argument for *lifting* the embargo to discourage Cuban support for revolution, than for keeping it in place to do so. Economic ties between Cuba and the United States would give the latter leverage and inducements that it does not now have to dissuade the Cubans.

Finally, if the embargo was originally imposed with a view to protecting the interests of U.S. property owners, it now has the opposite result. It is important that those citizens who lost properties in Cuba be compensated for that loss. Only in that way will the international principles which protect the holdings in one country of the citizens of another be upheld. But a compensation agreement must be accompanied by movement toward lifting the embargo, for while the Cubans recognize their inherent responsibility to compensate the U.S. owners (and in fact have already signed compensation agreements with every other country which has claims against Cuba), they argue on grounds of principle and pragmatism that they cannot do so until agreement is reached on raising the embargo. On principle, they portray the embargo as a form of economic aggression against them and say that so long as that aggression continues, they cannot be expected to pay compensation. On pragmatic grounds, because they do not have sufficient hard currency holdings to pay the compensation bill, they argue that this would have to be tied to earnings from renewed trade with the United States.

However one might contest the principle, the pragmatic argument is persuasive. Thus, if U.S. citizens are ever to receive compensation for their lost assets, a lifting of the embargo must be contemplated.

A final reason to remove the embargo has to do with the fact that the United States is presently one of the few countries in the international community not to trade with Cuba. This is an especially important point in Latin America, where the OAS removed impediments to trade relations with Cuba back in 1975. For the United States to hang onto this policy *ad infinitum* places it in the sole company of Pinochet's Chile and Stroessner's Paraguay. Rather than contributing to the isolation of Cuba, the embargo actually contributes more to the isolation of the United States.

To Dismantle the Embargo

The Foreign Assistance Act of 1961 authorized the President of the United States to establish and maintain an embargo on trade between the United States and Cuba. By the same authority, he has the power to lift it, either in part or totally, at any time. From the above, it is clear that its continued imposition no longer serves U.S. interests. On the contrary, several important objectives can be advanced by removing it, and, the compensation of U.S. citizens, can *only* be achieved in conjunction with its abrogation.

The embargo ought, then, to be lifted, but not as an isolated or unrelated act; rather, that must come about as part of a process, and must be directly tied to, a compensation agreement. If some U.S. administration of the future is prepared to approach the matter pragmatically and to begin a process of problem solving with Cuba, a sensible scenario might be the following:

1. In order to signal its readiness to begin such a process, the

United States might unilaterally lift the prohibition on the non-subsidized sale of foods and medicines to Cuba (which, on humanitarian grounds, many U.S. citizens feel never should have been imposed in the first place).

2. Having thus made a good-will gesture to get the ball rolling, the United States should suggest to Cuba that negotiations begin on a compensation agreement and on a timetable for lifting the embargo (see Section 5.1). Agreement on both issues would be announced simultaneously.

3. Having thus cleared the air and created an atmosphere more conducive to the constructive discussion of other outstanding issues, the two countries could establish a step-by-step agenda to conduct those discussions.

Notes

1. *Cuban Foreign Relations: a Chronology, 1959–1982.* A Center For Cuban Studies Publication, 1984. p.3–1960.

2. Ibid.

3. Ibid.

4. See Robbins, Carla Anne. *The Cuban Threat.* New York: McGraw Hill, 1982, pp.96–101.

5. *Cuban Foreign Relations*, p.5–1961.

6. Declaration of San Jose, August 28, 1960.

7. Ibid.

8. *The New York Times,* February 4, 1962, p.1.

9. Bonsal, Philip W. *Cuba, Castro and the United States.* Pittsburgh: University of Pittsburgh Press, 1971, p.135.

10. Losman, Donald L. *International Economic Sanctions, the Cases of Cuba, Israel, and Rhodesia* (University of Mexico Press, 1979).

11. Theriot, Lawrence H. *Cuba Faces the Economic Realities of the 1980s.* Study prepared for the use of the Joint Economic Committee of the Congress of the United States. March 22, 1982, p.11.

12. Perez-Lopez, Jorge F. "Cuban Economic Performance During 1981–1985; Prospects for 1986–1990," in *Cuba After the Third Party Congress—Selected Essays,* SAIS Johns Hopkins University Central American and Caribbean Program Occasional Paper No. 12, August 1986.

5.3   The Economic Issues
from Cuba's Perspective

Esteban Morales Dominguez
Hugo M. Pons Duarte

As aptly expressed by Cuban Vice Minister of Foreign Relations, Ricardo Alarcón, "The relations between Cuba and the United States since 1959 have been determined by Washington's reaction to the victorious Cuban Revolution and to the latter's repercussions in the rest of Latin America and the Caribbean."[1]

U.S. hostility to the Cuban Revolution was not long in coming. As early as January 9, 1959, the U.S. media began to criticize measures taken by the new government; *The New York Times,* for example, questioned the severe sentences against the war criminals of the Batista regime. This was only the beginning.

On May 17, 1959, Fidel Castro signed the Agrarian Reform Act, which simultaneously created the National Institute for Agrarian Reform. This brought the Cuban Revolution into direct conflict with U.S. interests. The U.S. response came on June 12, 1959, in the form of a diplomatic note, signed by Secretary of State Christian A. Herter, objecting to Cuba's decision to implement the Agrarian Reform Act. The note said in part: "The text of the Agrarian Reform Act is cause for great concern to the U.S. Government, with respect to the adequacy of the stipulations on compensating (U.S.) citizens, whose property may be subject to expropriation."[2]

The Cuban government, in responding to the U.S. note, said:

Unless the large estates are proscribed and the land redistributed appropriately, Cuba will continue to be an economically stagnant [country], with an increasing rate of unemployment. . . . The fundamental concern found in your note—with the complete list of the reservations and objections it contains—has to do with the form of payment adopted by Cuba's revolutionary government to compensate U.S. citizens whose property could be subject to expropriation in accordance with the agrarian act.[3]

The revolutionary government went on to explain that, although the 1940 Constitution stipulated that the price of exports be guaranteed in advance and paid in cash, Cuba found itself faced with a known surplus, a difficult economic situation that was characterized by the financial chaos into which Batista's tyrannical rule had thrown the country, and a considerable disparity in the balance of payments between Cuba and the United States, a situation that had been unfavorable to Cuba for the ten years that preceded the victory of the Revolution.

It added further that given the option of proscribing the large estates, and the obligation of restitution established in the Constitution, "the Revolutionary Government, in exercising the power vested in it by the Cuban people, who heroically rose up in arms against their oppressors . . . has chosen a way to provide restitution that, given the circumstances mentioned above, it judges more convenient for the paramount interests of the nation, which take precedence over all others, regardless of how worthy those others may be."[4]

And so it was that one of the conflicts arose in bilateral relations between the two nations—a conflict that still exists.

Cuba did, however, offer to make payments for the expropriated property at 4.5 percent annual interest, in 20-year bonds to be backed by the Cuban government.

Taking into consideration the obvious difficulties faced by the revolutionary government, some observers, noting U.S. concerns on the issue, recalled that the U.S. government had passed an agrarian reform law in Japan during the military occupation of that country—a law which had stipulated that compensation for the landowners would be paid in 24-year bonds at 3.5 percent annual interest. In view of that, why was so much pressure being brought to bear on Cuba? The answer is important in understanding the historic period that was opening in bilateral relations between Cuba and the United States. In challenging the historic interest the United States had in the island, Cuba's action went far beyond anything the United States had expected. The United States, indeed, had come to think of Cuba almost as an extension of its own territory and to assume that Cuban governments would accept dictates from Washington.

As Wayne Smith has noted: "In the view of many Americans, this brash upstart [Cuba] has dared to challenge the U.S., and has got away with it for almost twenty-five years. Such a view goes a long way toward explaining U.S. reaction to Cuba."[5] Given such an attitude, the hostile reaction of U.S. leaders following the triumph of the Cuban

Revolution is hardly surprising.

On January 8, 1960, for example, the *Washington Daily News* reported that a group of legal advisors to the U.S. government had recommended a reduction in the price the United States paid for Cuban sugar. Such a harsh blow would deprive Cuba of $150 million. This information appeared in a column written by Virginia Prewet and included the following recommendations from the government's advisors:

- Direct all litigation between the two countries to the Organization of American States.
- Resort to freezing all Cuban funds.
- Prohibit U.S. tourism in Cuba.
- Require cash payment for imports to Cuba, eliminating the traditional four-month grace period.

U.S. leaders had assumed, as God-given truth, that Cuba would always follow the path laid out for it by the United States. It became clear, however, with the advent of the Cuban Revolution, that in the heart of the Cuban people there was enough political strength to put an end, not only to U.S. power on the island, but to the umbilical cord that had tied Cuba to the United States for more than fifty years.

To understand the U.S. view of the options open to it in the post-1959 era, it is worth quoting the words of U.S. historian Robert Freeman Smith. In 1960, he wrote:

> The U.S. must choose the path it will follow in its relationship with Cuba. It can continue blindly following traditional policy and try to make the Cubans give in to force under the command of another Batista. But we can also work with the Cubans while they try to resolve their chronic problems . . . we can prove the sincerity of our national ideals, or we can confirm the persistent suspicions that we are merely another empire that tries to govern the world according to its own set of rules.[6]

As we know, the United States chose to respond with its traditional policy approach, confirming beyond a doubt, that, at least in its relations with Cuba, the United States was an empire that tried to rule the world according to its own set of rules. It only served to increase the tensions between the two nations. Wayne Smith, former head of the U.S. Interests Section in Havana, has said that the whole approach was afflicted by "intellectual sclerosis . . . that so distorts the perception of the Cuban problem . . . that no U.S. administration has come up with an effective policy toward Fidel Castro's Cuba."[7]

The break in relations and the economic blockade are inseparable incidents. They represent categorical examples of an imperialistic reaction on the part of the United States. And twenty years later, that attitude still lessens the chances of a possible improvement in relations between the two countries. Wayne Smith has noted: "The possibility of positively channeling U.S.-Cuban relations never materialized. The old image that the U.S. could unilaterally decide the future of Cuba was shattered. Proof of this, however, failed to prompt the U.S. to re-evaluate its ties with Cuba. The Cuban Revolution came as an unexpected and sad disappointment. But instead of seeking to creatively adapt to the new situation, U.S. leaders reacted in a way that made a practical compromise unthinkable."[8] For all these years, this has been the situation in America's policy toward Cuba.[9]

U.S. Economic Policy Toward Cuba Since the 1960s

The United States had always used its financial power and the sugar quota as a means of punishing or rewarding Cuba. The object of the policy, laid out by that country in the eighteenth century, was to keep the island from straying from its standard relations with the United States. And once again, these tactics were used. When the United States decided to end its Cuban sugar quota, following months of deteriorating relations between the two countries, it was primarily to punish Cuba.

The United States felt compelled to defend what had been the principal tenet of its policy toward Latin America and the Caribbean. Punishing Cuba would demonstrate to the other countries in the region that their well-being depended on "tight and friendly ties" with the neighbor to the north.

If we were to summarize U.S. economic policy toward Cuba over the last twenty-six years, we would characterize it as a series of coercive measures that exceeded continually the general standards of a commercial embargo. These measures, imposed both domestically and abroad, have always been aimed at preventing Cuba from consolidating its economy and gaining a foothold in the world economy.

Coercive Economic Measures the United States Has Imposed on Cuba

In its eagerness to create obstacles, and impede or prevent Cuba's economic development, the U.S. government has carried out a series of coercive economic measures with a political end in mind. The U.S.

government's initial policy toward Cuba took two approaches: fuel and sugar.

- In June 1960, the Texaco Oil Corporation, and subsequently ESSO and Shell, refused to process in their Cuban refineries the oil the Cuban government had begun to obtain from the Soviet Union. At the same time, in an effort to paralyze the island's economy, U.S. companies, under pressure from their government, were refusing to sell fuel to Cuba.
- In July 1960, acting under the authority of Presidential Proclamation 3355, the U.S. government reduced the imports of Cuban sugar to the U.S. market by 95 percent.[10] In reality, the imports were reduced to nothing, because the remaining 5 percent was made up of sugar that had already been certified to enter the country.

Following the escalation of these coercive actions, the U.S. government decided to suspend operation of its nickel factory in Oriente.

- In October 1960, the U.S. government began enforcing the measures it had passed, prohibiting exports from the United States to Cuba. Only food, medicine, and medical equipment were allowed, thus depriving the country of replacement parts to maintain the factories and equipment that had been bought on the U.S. market.
- December 16, 1960, following Presidential Proclamation 3383, again under the authority of the amended Sugar Act of 1948, the U.S. government suspended the Cuban sugar quota for the first three months of 1961.
- January 3, 1961, the U.S. government broke diplomatic and consular relations with the Cuban government, adding a finishing touch to the economic measures the United States had already taken against its island neighbor.
- March 31, 1961, following Presidential Proclamation 3401, also issued under the authority of the 1948 Sugar Act, the United States suspended the sugar quota for all of 1961.
- In September 1961, the U.S. Congress prohibited all assistance to the Cuban government and authorized the President to establish and maintain a blockade on all commerce between the United States and Cuba. Legislation allowing such an action was included in Section 620(a) of the 1961 Foreign Assistance Act.
- December 1, 1961, following Presidential Proclamation 3440, the United States suspended the Cuban sugar quota until June 30, 1962.

- On February 3, 1962, the U.S. president issued Presidential Proclamation 3447, which decreed an economic blockade to begin at 12:01 a.m., February 7, 1962. The decree included the following stipulations:

  It prohibited the United States from importing any goods that had originated in Cuba, as well as any goods imported from or through Cuba. The Secretary of the Treasury was directed to take any steps necessary to enforce this ruling, and the Secretary of Commerce was directed to carry through on the prohibition against U.S. exports to Cuba.[11]

- February 6, 1962, a total embargo on Cuban exports to the United States was imposed.[12]
- In March 1962, Section 5(b) of the 1917 Trading with the Enemy Act was amended to prohibit the importation of any product fabricated completely or in part from Cuban materials, even if manufactured in other countries.
- In May 1962, the U.S. Treasury Department promulgated Treasury Order 55638, under the authority of Section 401 of the 1962 Tariff Classification Act and the 1951 Trade Agreement Expansion Act, as modified by the Trade Expansion Act of 1962. The new order unilaterally rescinded Cuba's *Most Favored Nation Status* and the preference formerly accorded it under the GATT agreement, to which both countries were signatories.
- In September 1962, the U.S. government announced that all ships involved in trade with Cuba, no matter what their country of registry, would be blacklisted and prohibited from entering U.S. ports.

These blockade measures taken against Cuba put the revolutionary government in a difficult situation in the world market.

- First, Cuba found itself forced to trade with distant regions. This of course raised the price of its exports and imports. Cuba's exports were made less competitive, and imports to Cuba created tremendous balance of payment deficits.
- Second, Cuba was placed at a disadvantage in the world shipping market in the sense that it had to comply with certain stipulations that were rarely applied elsewhere. For example, Cuba was forced to pay premiums above the prevailing rates in the shipping market.
- In June 1963, the Cuban Assets Control Regulations were issued. Approved July 8, they revoked the Cuban Import Regulations, and prohibited all transactions carried out by the Cuban

government, its representatives or its citizens. The new rules blocked any individual, partnership or other group of individuals from making transfers of payment or credit, from conducting foreign exchange transactions, and from importing or exporting money, gold, silver, or any other precious metals between the United States and Cuba. The new rules blocked all assets in the United States belonging to Cuba or Cuban nationals, froze bank accounts, and prohibited any transaction involving the affected property. The measures of the economic blockade were enforced to the full extent of the law.

In February 1964, the U.S. Commerce Department eliminated butter from the scanty list of U.S. products Cuba was still allowed to purchase. Cuba had been a traditional buyer of surplus U.S. butter, an arrangement that had benefitted the meat industry, of which butter was a by-product, because there was not much demand for butter on the U.S. market. Therefore, U.S. producers were also affected by the action taken against Cuba.

The U.S. Economic Blockade of Cuba and Fluctuations in Bilateral Relations

From 1960 until the present, the U.S. embargo has been inflexibly in place against Cuba. There have been ebbs and flows, however, in the political relations between the two countries. Immediately after John F. Kennedy's inauguration in 1961, for example, he accepted his predecessor's plan to invade Cuba with an army of Cuban exiles, armed and trained by the United States. But subsequently, in 1963, President Kennedy sent President Fidel Castro a message that seemed to indicate the possibility of an official rapprochement between the two governments. Perhaps the assassination of the U.S. leader left unfinished what might have been the beginning of a certain detente between the two nations.

From that moment until the Nixon administration, the United States took a position that ruled out any effort to better relations with Cuba. Nevertheless, other nations in Latin America began to change their attitudes toward Cuba, as evidenced in the policies of Jamaica, Panama, Peru, and Argentina, among others.

On July 28, 1975, the Organization of American States voted to end political and economic sanctions against Cuba. This action formally opened the way for each member nation to determine for itself whether it would have diplomatic and trade relations with Cuba, which some of those nations had already begun to establish.

Despite the OAS decision, the United States continued to maintain its blockade of Cuba, with only a slight modification: foreign subsidiaries of U.S. companies were no longer prohibited from exporting goods to Cuba. True, the Nixon and Ford administrations also began a series of informal discussions with the Cuban government, but these broke down in late 1975 because of sharply conflicting views regarding the situation in Angola.

With the inauguration of Jimmy Carter in 1977, the prospects for some improvement in U.S.-Cuban relations seemed to brighten. In March and April of 1977, the first formal negotiations between U.S. and Cuban diplomats were conducted in New York and Havana, respectively, and a fishing agreement and maritime boundary agreement were signed. On September 1 that same year, moreover, the two sides reinstituted limited diplomatic communications by setting up interests sections in one another's capitals.

Before further progress could be made, the warming trend was blocked by U.S. demands that, as a precondition for improved relations with the United States, Cuba take certain steps which would have gone against its principles, and which, in any event, were matters for multilateral, not bilateral, decision. One of the most important of these was the demand that Cuba remove its troops from Angola—a demand that was voiced even at times when South African troops were deep in Angolan territory. The United States did not take Angolan security into account; it simply demanded that Cuban troops leave. This was unrealistic and of course was rejected by Cuba.

By the end of the Carter presidency, in January of 1981, U.S.-Cuban relations had so deteriorated that tensions were, if anything, even higher than when Carter had taken office.

Carter was replaced by Ronald Reagan, who instituted the most hostile policy against Cuba since the invasion at the Bay of Pigs. Despite conciliatory signals from Cuba, the new U.S. administration announced a tightening of the embargo and a a series of other punitive measures against Cuba.

According to Charles Redman, a spokesman for the Secretary of State: "These measures will make it that much more difficult for the Cuban Government to obtain dollars from the U.S., and to illegally obtain American products. The object is to stiffen compliance with the embargo, denying the Castro regime economic benefits from the U.S. for as long as Castro continues to ignore his *international obligations and to maintain a policy that is contrary to U.S. interests.*"[13]

As one can see, the Reagan administration's measures are guided by objectives that go beyond earlier U.S. intentions toward Cuba. The restrictions were stated in such a general way that the United States could interpret at its pleasure what it deemed to be Cuba's international obligations, and what it interpreted as Cuban actions that ran contrary to U.S. interests. Should Cuba ever be prepared to accept such U.S. demands (something it will never do), it would have to begin by asking Washington precisely what those demands are. The Reagan administration has taken its policy of blockade, aggression, and harassment against Cuba to such extremes that it no longer knows how to phrase its demands. They seem to be infinite in their scope—and, thus, unanswerable.

Compensation and Embargo

Historically, the issue of compensation to U.S. property owners has been tied to the blockade the United States imposed on Cuba. Cuba has not, in principle, refused to pay compensation for U.S. property nationalized by the revolutionary government. But, with the severance of ties between the two countries and the imposition of the blockade, negotiations over this controversial aspect of U.S.-Cuban relations were left unattended.

When Cuba's sugar quota was abolished, it was Eisenhower who said: "This action represents economic sanctions against Castro. Now we must look ahead to other moves—economic, diplomatic, strategic . . ."[14] The revolutionary government had already warned the U.S. administration of the consequences of this type of action. But the U.S. government underestimated Cuba's capacity to respond.

When Cuba nationalized the property of U.S. companies operating in Cuba, the following companies were the most affected: The Cuban Telephone Company (owned by ITT and ATT), the Cuban Electric Company (owned by a subsidiary of the American Bond and Share Company of New York), the refineries of the Standard Oil Company of New Jersey, and Texaco Inc., and the fuel distribution network of the Sinclair Oil Company. In addition, the revolutionary government nationalized thirty-six U.S. sugar refineries.

In order to reimburse the owners of the property nationalized by the revolutionary government, Cuba had planned to issue bonds that could be repaid out of Cuba's annual export to the United States. It was thought that the necessary funds would be equal to about 25 percent of exports to the United States, which exceeded three million tons, at a price that never went below 5.4 cents a pound.[15] But compensation payments could not begin until the United States restored Cuba's sugar quota, thus providing the Cuban government with the wherewithal to make the payments.

Rather than considering restoration, however, the U.S. government escalated to new levels its offensive against Cuba, decreeing the blockade and a policy of isolation. The U.S. State Department announced that the embargo had been imposed to "defend the legitimate economic interests of the citizens of this country against the aggressive, injurious and discriminatory policy of Castro's regime."[16]

The Cuban government reacted by expropriating the remaining 166 pieces of U.S. property in Cuba. They included the Nicaro Nickel Plant, Woolworth's, Sears and Roebuck, the General Electric Company, Westinghouse, Remington-Rand, and Coca-Cola, as well as some hotels and bond companies.

The U.S. owners of property in Cuba, instead of resisting their government's policies, adopted positions and attitudes that placed them in sharp confrontation with the Cuban government. The U.S. refineries, for example, may have believed they were serving the interests of their country by refusing to process Soviet oil. In reality, they were opposing the interests of the country that had served them as a source of profits for years.

Possibility of Solutions

Perhaps after all these years, attitudes on the U.S. side have begun to change. Since the middle of the 1970s, some affiliates of U.S. companies located in third companies have agreed to trade with Cuba. An appreciable number of businesspeople have visited Cuba, and new and more flexible ideas seem to be taking root. A number of U.S. citizens now insist that it is useless and inappropriate to maintain an economic blockade against Cuba. Furthermore, Cuba's potential as a nearby market makes it attractive to a number of U.S. companies.

Hence, we believe that a search for solutions to the issues of both the blockade and compensation may soon become feasible. It is our opinion that such advances would require the following:

1. The existence of a U.S. administration that is prepared to negotiate with Cuba on issues based on a bilateral agenda.[17] Lifting the embargo would be one of those issues for urgent discussion.

2. While such negotiations are in progress, we believe that Cuba would not be unwilling to allow a few U.S. companies that are really interested in dealing with Cuba to discuss that possibility even before the blockade is removed. The possibility also exists that Cuba and the U.S. companies might enter into talks on the issue of compensation.

3. Negotiations between the two governments to determine a fair compensation figure—one which would take into account a) damages

to the Cuban economy caused by U.S. punitive measures; and b) the exaggerated claims of many U.S. companies, some of which placed a value on their properties that was many times what, for tax purposes, they had previously said those same properties were worth. These calculations should also take into account the fact that some U.S. companies had actually been operating in violation of Cuban law.

4. Some sensible formula for payment of the compensation figure thus established.

The above are only suggestions. Clearly, before Cuba could carry through on such measures, it would have to assess thoroughly all aspects of the developing relationship with the United States. What is clear, however, is that through these or other devices, solutions could be found to the economic aspects of the U.S-Cuban dispute, just as solutions could be found to its other aspects.

Notes

1. Alarcón, Ricardo. "Cuba and the U.S.: Two Perspectives." *Relations between Cuba and the U.S.: Standards of Behavior and Options,* edited and compiled by Juan G. Tokatlian. Bogotá: CEREC, 1984, p.22.

2. *Bohemia Magazine,* June 21, 1959, p.76.

3. Ibid, pp.42–43.

4. Ibid, p.77.

5. Smith, Wayne S. "U.S.-Cuban Relations: Guidelines and Alternatives," in Juan C. Tokatlian (ed.), *Cuba and the U.S.: Two Perspectives,* p.31.

6. Smith, Robert Freeman. *The U.S. and Cuba: Negotiations and Diplomacy, 1917–1960.* Buenos Aires, Argentina: Editorial Palestra, 1965, p.26.

7. Smith, Wayne S. "Washington-Havana: Short-sighted Diplomacy." Caracas: *Revista Nueva Sociedad* (November–December 1982), p.21.

8. Smith, "Washington-Havana: Short-sighted Diplomacy," pp.14–15.

9. Except, as we shall see, to some extent in the first two years of Democratic President James Carter's administration.

10. Presidential Proclamation 3355 was issued under the authority conferred on the President by Section 408 of the 1948 Sugar Act, as amended July 6, 1960, by Public Law 86-592. The amended legislation provides that the President shall determine, notwithstanding any other provision of the Sugar Act, the quota for Cuba for the balance of calendar year 1960 and for the three-month period ending March 31, 1961, "in such amount or amounts as he shall find from time to time to be in the national interest."

11. Stipulated in the 1949 Export Control Act, amended (Sections 2021–2032 of Title 50, U.S. Code of National Defense and War).

12. Issued under the authority of Section 620(a)1 of the 1961 Foreign Assistance Act, and Presidential Proclamation 3447, which stipulated its promulgation.

13. USIS Report. Text of Presidential Proclamation on Cuban Immigration to the United States, Washington, D.C., August 22, 1986.

14. Quoted in Thomas, Hugh. *Cuba: The Pursuit of Freedom*. London, Harper & Row: 1971, p.1289.

15. Phillips, R. Hart. "Castro Decrees Seizure of Rest of U.S. Property: Cites Cut in Sugar Quota." *New York Times* (August 8, 1960).

16. "Text of U.S. Announcement of Embargo." the *New York Times* (October 20, 1960.)

17. Though that is not to say that Cuba would refuse to discuss even multilateral issues with the U.S. See, for example, Fidel Castro's statement of July 28, 1983, in which he indicated Cuba's willingness to discuss the Central American issue with the United States and to play a constructive role in the search for peace.

6

THE PROBLEM OF
THE GUANTÁNAMO NAVAL BASE

6.1   The Base from the
U.S. Perspective

Wayne S. Smith

Historical Background

Established in 1903 as a coaling station to help the fleet protect the approaches to the future Panama Canal, the United States naval base at Guantánamo Bay, on Cuba's southeastern coast, is the oldest U.S. military installation outside the continental United States. The original leasing agreement was signed in February of 1903, and was based on a paragraph in the Platt Amendment attached to the Cuban Constitution of 1901 which stated:

> That to enable the United States to maintain the independence of Cuba, and to protect the people thereof, as well as its own defense, the government of Cuba will sell or lease to the United States lands necessary for coaling and Naval stations at certain specified points to be agreed upon by the President of the United States.

The United States at first indicated its intention to use this paragraph to acquire another naval facility at Bahia Honda, on Cuba's northwestern coast. These plans were eventually shelved, however, leaving Guantánamo as the only base leased by the United States as a result of the Platt Amendment.

Cubans have long argued, with some reason, that the Platt Amendment was forced on them by the United States as the price for ending U.S. military occupation of the island, and, therefore, that the 1903 base agreement was invalid. Whatever substance there may have been to this argument, it was undone when, following the abrogation of the Platt Amendment in 1934, Cuba signed a new treaty that same year reaffirming the original base agreement and giving the United States indefinite lease to the land and water that make up the base.

The 1934 treaty, which is still in force, acknowledges that ultimate sovereignty remains with Cuba, but specifies that the agreement can only be abrogated or modified with the consent of both parties. There is *no* ninety-nine-year clause, as is widely assumed in the United States.

When Fidel Castro assumed power in January of 1959, one of the new revolutionary government's first acts was to give assurances that it would respect all existing international treaties. This, of course, included the treaty of 1934 covering the Guantánamo base. Thus, whatever the political arguments may be, the juridical foundation for continued U.S. occupancy is sound.

Existing Situation

Guantánamo is the only U.S. base maintained within the territory of a communist country. The Castro government has never mounted a serious military move to seize the base. During the first years of Castro's rule, however, there were numerous incidents around its perimeter as U.S. Marines and Cuban frontier guards exchanged insults, and sometimes bullets. Casualties and several deaths resulted. To reduce those incidents, Castro, in 1965, moved the Cuban defense line a quarter of a mile back from their fence, leaving a no-man's land of that width between the Marines and the frontier guards, who continue to face one another from the respective bunkers. Inside the perimeter, the base is also defended by the largest mine field in the world.

Embracing some 45 square miles of land and water, the base sits astride the entrance to Guantánamo Bay, which runs through the base and then opens out in Cuban territory. Several Cuban ports are situated on the bay, and as the 1934 treaty provides for free passage, Cuban and Soviet vessels, as well as those of other countries, regularly pass through the base on their way to and from these ports.

Guantánamo is now used principally as a training station for the Atlantic fleet, providing support facilities for some 80 to 100 vessels per year engaged in shakedown cruises and exercises of other kinds. Its near-perfect weather, minimal sea and air traffic, and established repair facilities, make it the navy's best such warm-water station. The base includes a naval air station, though the fact that the air strip ends so close to the base perimeter makes landing and taking off a tricky business.

Some 6,500 people now live on the base, including about 2,500 military personnel, their dependents, and civilian employees of several nationalities. The base is entirely self-sufficient, with its own water plant, schools, transportation, and entertainment facilities.

A dwindling number of Cuban commuters still enter from C territory each morning and depart each evening. All worked a base prior to the Revolution and have been permitted by the Castro government to continue their employment. Though once numbering in the hundreds, there are now only about fifty left, and soon all will have retired or died. By and large, the Cuban workers have been replaced by Jamaicans, who contract to work periods of time at the base.

As the U.S. sees it, the naval base at Guantánamo Bay serves a useful purpose, and it has a legal right, based on the treaty of 1934, to continue its operation.

As Cuba sees it, the naval base is on its sovereign territory and is unwelcome. Further, given the tense relations between the two countries, Cuba cannot help but see the base as a foothold from which the United States might launch some aggression against it.

In sum, Cuba wants the United States to withdraw and turn control of the base over to Cuba. The United States refuses.

A Possible Solution

What seems an insoluble problem might, however, under somewhat changed circumstances, find a workable solution. For one thing, while the base is *useful* to the United States, it is by no means *vital* or indispensable. U.S. arguments that it is both these things can be seen simply as part of the public relations effort to bolster its juridical position and keep U.S. public opinion behind its determination to hang onto Guantánamo. The effort is perfectly understandable, but the substance of the argument—that the base is vital to us—does not stand up to careful analysis. One can hardly define a "training" facility as *vital* to our defense, especially as there are other nearby naval bases—in Puerto Rico, for example—to which Guantánamo's support mission could be transferred. In short, the United States could give up Guantánamo, with some inconvenience, but without significant damage to the U.S. security posture.

Further, maintaining a military base on foreign soil against the will of the government and people of the affected country is neither helpful to our image internationally nor cost-effective militarily. Not only is Guantánamo not vital, in other words, but there could be compensating gains involved in giving it up—should changing conditions ever make that possible.

All that being said, however, the hard fact remains that under present conditions, the United States *cannot* return the base. Given the tense, adversarial relationship with Cuba, and the fact that Cuba is the military ally of its principal global rival, the Soviet Union, the United States cannot simply hand it over to the Castro government. One does not give a valuable military asset to an adversary at the same time that one is involved in a continuing confrontation with that adversary, even if the cost of hanging onto it is high.

But assuming the sort of strategic decision presupposed in the Preface to this volume—that is, one leading to a gradual reduction of tensions and the step-by-step resolution of problems between the United States and Cuba—new possibilities might open up for a solution of the base issue. Since there would have to be much more confidence between the two than now exists, the warming trend would have to be fairly well advanced before the base problem could even be considered. But at that point—let us say after a number of other contentious issues had been handled satisfactorily and after diplomatic relations had been resumed—the United States could then agree to begin discussions concerning the base's future. How far these discussions could go would depend upon progress in improving the overall relationship, that is, of taking it out of a confrontational context. Objectively, once the confrontational edge between the two countries had been removed, there would be no reason that a satisfactory formula for the base's return could not be worked out.

Little would be gained from trying to elaborate specific formulae in this chapter—better to leave that to future negotiating teams. Suffice it to say here that:

1. This would be a major concession on the part of the United States. For it to be politically feasible even under the best of circumstances would require some matching move on the other side. One such gesture might be agreement on the part of Cuban and Soviet authorities not to deploy to Cuba in the future Bear reconnaissance aircraft or other such systems.

2. An indispensable condition, whatever the specific formula, would be a guarantee that the base not be used by Soviet forces. This should not prove difficult to secure. The Soviets have privately indicated their willingness to keep hands off the base if that would facilitate its return to Cuba, and fulfillment of that condition would not be difficult to verify.

3. What might lead to even faster agreement would be a guarantee on Cuba's part that the base, once in Cuban hands, would not be used for military purposes at all; rather, that it would be transformed into a civilian facility. The non-use of Guantánamo by both Cuban and Soviet naval vessels could be easily monitored and verified. Further,

such an arrangement ought to be acceptable to Cuba, since adequate facilities already exist in Cienfuegos and Santiago to service the naval vessels of Cuba—as well as those of the Soviet Union. And, finally, a civilian facility could be most useful in the development of the Guantánamo region, one of Cuba's poorest.

Interim Steps

Even before agreeing to begin negotiations for the return of the base, both sides could take measures to reduce tensions related to its presence. The United States, for example, could refrain from bringing in vessels bearing nuclear weapons and could endeavor to cut to a minimum the number of violations of Cuban airspace committed by planes taking off or landing at the base, or conducting exercises there —for example, carrier-based planes conducting dive-bombing runs. The United States might also begin to reduce the number of base personnel.

For its part, Cuba could halt harassing flights and begin to permit some access by land. As it is now, only the few Cuban commuter workers are allowed to leave or enter from the land side. The base is totally self-sufficient and has no contact with the country in which it is located. Under changed circumstances, it would be a convenience if it could again begin to buy some of its provisions from Cuban suppliers, even if only on a temporary basis. Before departing, moreover, many base personnel would like to see what is on the other side of the fence. Perhaps ways could be found to permit limited numbers to visit Santiago—or even Havana—as tourists.

Final Words

The mechanics of returning the Guantánamo Naval Base to Cuban control would be complicated. Even without going into the details of such an arrangement, however, what is clear from the above is that even in the case of this most difficult bilateral problem, a solution acceptable to both sides could be worked out, once the two governments put their minds to it.

6.2 Cuba's National Security and the Question of the Guantánamo Naval Base _____

_____ Rafael Hernández Rodriguez

Let us imagine a hypothetical country on the northern border of the United States; that this mythical country's population grew to 5.5 billion; its armed forces to 30 million and its defense budget to $40 trillion; that the sophisticated equipment of this powerful state included 3,000 attack submarines, more than 50,000 combat airplanes, and a giant nuclear arsenal—all pointing at the United States, which had yet to acquire the atomic bomb; that the United States had also to reckon with a naval base on U.S. territory that covered an area three times the size of the state of Rhode Island. Let's suppose this country posed a hostile military threat to the United States, including the possibility of a direct attack; that it had tried in various ways to overthrow the government of the United States, sending in an expedition of U.S. exiles and making more than ten assassination attempts against the U.S. president; that this country to the north had surrounded the United States with numerous military bases and facilities, whose forces were expressly deployed against the United States; that not only had it cut off bilateral trade, but that it had put pressure on its allies in the rest of the world in an effort to isolate the United States in its relations with other nations; and that finally, in this asymmetrical tableau, this country to the north insisted on continually reporting the danger the United States represented to its national security.

What weight would the United States put on preparing for its defense? What measures would the United States take to protect itself? How would it respond to the offer of economic and military assistance from a country in another hemisphere, a country the same size as the hostile neighbor to the north?

Many writers emphasize the extent to which the Cuban dilemma affects U.S. security; fewer analyze the tremendous burden the United States puts on Cuba's legitimate national security. Obviously, only a perspective that fully considers the significant weight of Cuba's national security concerns can offer an accurate view of the present situation. This framework is essential when examining the issue of the Guantánamo Naval Base.

Cuba's National Security Agenda

The essence of Cuba's national security concerns flows from the possibility of a direct attack from the United States, whether against military or economic targets, of a blockade, of a massive surprise air strike on Cuba's main cities, or of an invasion. The agreement between the USSR and the United States, which brought an end to the October 1962 crisis, established a compromise that the United States would not attack Cuba as long as the medium-range nuclear missiles were removed from Cuban territory. Cuba did not participate in this agreement, but subsequently accepted its value in keeping the peace and preventing Cuba from having to sacrifice its basic political tenets at a time when the country faced one of its greatest risks.[1] In 1970, 1978, and 1979, the United States raised the possibility that the agreement had been violated, citing the supposed presence of "offensive arms" in Cuba. Each time, it was shown that neither Cuba's weapons nor its military collaboration with the Soviets were threatening U.S. security.

In spite of these historical precedents, new questions have arisen in U.S. political power circles. Thus, in the Kissinger Report, and even in President Reagan's statements,[2] Cuba is accused of not respecting the agreement, thus implying that the United States has been relieved of its commitment not to attack Cuba. In a related development, the area around the island has been the scene of naval and air maneuvers, particularly since 1980. As Administration representatives have said—Alexander Haig, in 1982—these air force and navy exercises are not only directed against revolutionary movements in Central America and the Caribbean, they also serve as a sort of "sanitary cordon" around Cuba, in case the United States should invade El Salvador or Nicaragua. In addition to the SR-71 reconnaissance flights over and around the island, Cuban airspace is violated by flights out of the Guantánamo Naval Base.[3] As one can see, U.S. lack of consistency in observing the understanding of 1962 offers no firm guarantee to Cuba's national security.

A second fundamental aspect of Cuba's concern for its national security is the threat posed by terrorism. As we have pointed out,

Cuba has been the object, over the years, of counter-revolutionary activities, either sponsored or tolerated by U.S. security agencies. Diplomats—as in the case of Félix García (1980) in New York—have been the subject of criminal attacks, as have Cubans who are living abroad, such as Carlos Muñiz and Eulalio Negrín (1979). The Cuban government has offered the U.S. government information on the activities of these terrorists. Ironically, Cuba was listed as one of the five main potential targets of U.S. reprisals, planned in response to supposed terrorist acts against the United States in 1985.

As part of the supposedly covert activities carried out by the United States, spies have infiltrated the island and plans have been implemented for the assassination of President Fidel Castro and other leaders. According to the Senate Intelligence Committee, back in 1975, there had been at least eight attempts to assassinate Fidel Castro. In 1981, at the 68th Interparliamentary Conference in Havana, Cuba accused the CIA of once again carrying out attempts against the lives of Cuban leaders.[4]

Piracy is another relevant issue, characterized by the different illegal actions taken by counter-revolutionary groups and individuals. Airplane highjacking taxed Cuba in the years that followed the revolution. Since then, however, as has happened to other aspects of the U.S. policy of destabilization, the tables have been turned[5]; air piracy has begun to plague the United States. When faced with such incidents, Cuba penalized the highjackers, as dictated by international law. But the United States has historically welcomed the highjackers of Cuban vessels, thus encouraging these illegal practices and endangering the life and limb of Cuban citizens; so Cuban fishing boats have become the victims of a piracy that is either sponsored or tolerated by U.S. maritime authorities and security agencies, and by members of the counter-revolutionary forces. Although recently some highjackers have been prosecuted, the main attitude among the bureaucrats of the current administration has generally encouraged highjacking and piracy.

Another aspect of this campaign of harassment is the introduction, often criticized by Cuba, of diseases that plague plants, animals, and people. Given Cuba's proximity to the United States and its common border with the Guantánamo Naval Base, this type of action becomes relatively easy to implement and difficult for Cuban security forces to detect. Generally speaking, the effects of environmental contamination constitute a problem for Cuba's national security in light of the country's geographic vulnerability and its proximity, both to the straits of Florida and the southern United States. A recent exchange of letters, between President Fidel Castro and Congressman Michael Bilirakis of

Florida, emphasized the need for mutual protection from the area's nuclear power plants. The existence of a considerable number of these facilities on U.S. territory, and the climatic conditions of that region, permanently expose Cuba to any contamination, whether it be nuclear or of another type that could reach the island on the winds from the north.

It is obvious that when the entire range of Cuba's security concerns are tallied and sharpened by the attitude of the present U.S. administration, it does not create a stable environment for constructive dialogue, nor a climate that inspires in Cuba a confident attitude. Furthermore, those concerns have a permanent impact on the country's economy and on its social development. The tremendous defense and security costs, in terms of both labor and resources, act as an inevitable drag on the indices that measure the nations's quality of life. The relative detente of the 1970s allowed a 50 percent reduction in military personnel.[6] In the 1980s, on the other hand, the cost to society of supporting the military sector had to be increased. Under the new guidelines stated in *The War of All the People*, the armed forces have been streamlined in an effort to cut down the use of resources on which the economy is dependent. Nevertheless, the more than one million reserves and one and one-half million militiamen, all of whom have had to be trained and equipped, as well as the thousands of other persons involved in civil defense activities, provide a measure of the social costs of Cuba's defense. It has been calculated that 80 percent of those Cubans who are physically fit for combat have been mobilized, regardless of their age.[7] At a time when Cuba faces a calamitous economic climate abroad, its critical priorities have been to modernize its weaponry and to make the investments necessary to guarantee wartime production, provide civilian shelters and, in general, to prepare the country for the threat of an attack.

It could be reasoned that the goal of the United States is, precisely, to maintain this vexing situation as a permanent reality, with the resulting damage to Cuba's socio-economic development. But the same examples mentioned above illustrate that the threat is counterproductive for U.S. policy toward Cuba since it encourages cohesion within the country and stirs popular support. Cuba's policy, on the other hand, offers no alternatives in this regard. The purpose of the country's accelerated defense build-up in recent years has been to serve as a deterrent, since an attack against Cuba would have very grave socio-economic consequences, while simultaneously creating a threat to international peace.

We have summarized some of the identifiable elements of Cuba's national security agenda within the framework of its bilateral relations with the United States. It should be noted that many of those security concerns are, directly or indirectly, linked to the presence of the Guantánamo Naval Base. The base exists more in the interest of a policy than in the interest of U.S. national security, as we will try to show in the following section.

The Guantánamo Naval Base Within the Framework of U.S. and Cuban Interests: Security and Policy

Even U.S. military authors have been among those emphasizing the need to develop a framework for negotiating with Cuba in the interest of U.S. national security.[8] It has been stated that the United States should initiate a policy aimed at reducing the Soviet military presence, and that the way to do so in the long run is to normalize relations with Cuba. In general terms, this statement says that an inflexible policy that emphasizes force does irreparable damage to the U.S. position. It concludes that the greatest danger of a "static" policy toward Cuba, one based on displays of strength and pure military muscle, could lead to the "eventual loss of the Guantánamo Base to the Soviet navy."[9] This idea, which could well be called the *Cam Ranh Syndrome*, appears as part of a larger account of U.S. focus on the Caribbean Basin, and particularly on Cuba.[10] We'll return to it again.

Let us quickly examine a few U.S. opinions on the value and the function of the Guantánamo Base, as well as the different ways in which the conflict between the United States and Cuba has been handled.

Some authors have asserted that the base "has rapidly lost its utility and is consequently vulnerable," which makes its return "not too high a price to pay" when negotiating the Soviet presence in Cuba.[11] In fact, during the October Crisis, the U.S. Ambassador to the U.N., Adlai Stevenson, suggested using the Guantánamo Base as part of a plan to demilitarize, neutralize, and guarantee Cuba's territorial integrity. This was based on the idea that Guantánamo was worth very little. President Kennedy's response, it's interesting to note, was that given *the existing situation,* it was not possible to consider the return of Guantánamo. (The emphasis is mine.)

Given the changing nature of U.S. defense needs, it has been pointed out that U.S. policy would allow for either the modification of Guantánamo's status to give Cuba a role in it, or the return of the base to Cuba, using it to negotiate certain concessions from that country.[12] The base no longer plays a strategic role and most of its functions and facilities have in fact been duplicated nearby at the Roosevelt Roads

Base in Puerto Rico. Some sources have asserted that the base is more of a symbol in that it does not pose much of a threat to Cuba, nor does it offer a secure situation for the United States.[13] From a strictly military point of view, the base is not seen as playing a vital role, although for the navy's purposes, it has been useful, both as a vantage point from which to survey the Caribbean's sea lanes, and as a limited training facility for operations in tropical climates.

The U.S. Naval Base at Guantánamo serves as training and preparation site for the Atlantic Fleet. It also serves as a control point over the area that extends from the United States to the Caribbean channel—particularly the Gulf of Mexico, the U.S. eastern seaboard, and the Windward, the Mona, and the Anegada Passages. The base would theoretically play a role, should there be a blockade of Cuba, because of its location. Generally speaking, however, the vulnerability of the base, with its scanty crew, suggests that its role is not vital to U.S. plans.

The base, for example, has played no role at all in U.S. military actions in the Basin, such as the 1965 invasion of the Dominican Republic or the 1983 invasion of Grenada.

It must also be recognized that the advantages of the base's location, with its deep waters and the possibility it offers of speedy access to maneuver sites, are not comparable to the tactical and strategic advantages of other facilities. The Waters of Guantánamo, bounded as they are by Haiti, Jamaica, and the Grand Cayman Island, pose limitations that prevent it from favorable comparison to the area north of Puerto Rico and in the arc of the Lesser Antilles, where the United States carries out a range of exercises.

Surveillance and control of the area to the south and the east of the United States are already being carried out from other U.S. bases, such as Roosevelt Roads, the bases in the Panama Canal Zone, and even those in Florida, at Key West and Jacksonville. Their role is enhanced by the hydro-accoustic detection center in the Bahamas, where the Atlantic Undersea Test Evaluation Center (AUTEC) is located, and by air force bases such as McDill and Homestead in Florida, which conduct air and naval surveillance.

Moreover, the placement of battle groups led by carriers or battleships, such as those that protect the ports in the Gulf of Mexico, emphasize the navy's capacity to re-deploy its forces among the bases on U.S. territory.[14] It's no secret that the main mission of the naval bases in this area of the Gulf is to control, police, and spy on Cuba.

In summary, the base's tasks have either been duplicated elsewhere, or they can be replaced by the chain of naval bases located along the Gulf or Atlantic coasts of the United States. The bases at

Norfolk, Jacksonville, Charleston, Key West, Pensacola, and other sites along the inner Gulf, without even mentioning the bases in Puerto Rico, could accomplish all the tasks now carried out by the Base at Guantánamo. As U.S. naval dispositions at these other bases have become stronger, the relative importance of Guantánamo has diminished.

If the contingency plans for Cuba, or for any other of the Caribbean or Central American countries, could go ahead without the Guantánamo Base, then it is obvious that its main function is a political one: To maintain this symbol of U.S. power in the Caribbean; to hold a card with which to obtain future concessions from Cuba; and, as recently acknowledged by President Reagan himself, to impose the U.S. presence, even against the expressed will of the Cuban people.[15]

For Cuba, the base has been and continues to be a source of irritation and provocation. It is a known fact that the base has historically sheltered counter-revolutionaries, and in certain cases, been the planning site for attacks on Cuba. Although the crimes against workers and border guards that took place in the 1960s have not been repeated, there is nothing to say they could not occur again—if only by accident—thus becoming again a source of tension. It is not by chance that, in this last period of the Reagan administration, such incidents have increased markedly. In the past, Cuba's policy has been to act only with prudence and forethought, taking care not to stir up patriotic fervor over the Base at Guantánamo. But the mere existence of the base, and its continued provocations, make it an area of permanent conflict.

This analysis has focused on examining the national security concerns that arise out of the question of Guantánamo. There is no reason to delve into the legal aspects, which have been covered by other authors.[16] The base is the heritage of the Treaty of Reciprocity of 1903. It was retained by the United States in the Relationship Treaty of 1934, signed by the Caffery-Batista-Mendieta government and the Roosevelt Administration. If the first treaty was conceived within the framework of U.S. intervention in Cuba, and with the backing of the Platt Amendement, the second kept the Platt spirit by establishing a spurious condition: "To lease in perpetuity" a territory that was successively widened beyond the site of the original coal station on Guantánamo Bay. As we have noted, this idea is inherently contradictory to the main point of a leasing agreement, which is temporary per se. The "lease in perpetuity" of Guantánamo contradicts the inalienable right of sovereignty that Cuba has to maintain its territory intact. Furthermore, the U.S. hold on Guantánamo runs contrary to the law that governs treaties between nations. That law

Number of Incidents at the Guantanamo Naval Base

Provocations	1959	1960	1961	1962	1963	1964	1965	1966	1967	1968	1869	1970	1971	1972
Pointing weapons	0	0	0	222	98	155	87	100	9	9	3	0	1	0
Shots fired	0	0	0	309	71	88	169	79	2	0	0	0	0	0
Killed and wounded	0	0	0	0	0	3	6	1	0	0	0	0	0	0
Violating Cuban waters	0	1	0	953	75	15	62	26	52	14	21	25	8	26
Violating Cuban air space	64	82	74	4912	524	112	58	15	56	47	107	62	51	45
Violating Cuban territory	0	0	0	21	365	101	26	20	5	10	6	6	0	0
Throwing objects	0	0	0	236	439	600	40	0	2	4	0	0	0	1
Obscene acts	0	0	0	17	3	3	3	0	0	0	0	0	0	2
Verbal insults	0	0	0	488	363	316	121	17	5	1	0	1	0	4

Provocations	1973	1974	1975	1976	1977	1978	1979	1980	1981	1982	1983	1984	1985
Pointing weapons	1	2	9	2	1	0	0	2	2	3	28	4	0
Shots fired	2	0	2	0	1	0	0	4	0	1	6	2	0
Killed and wounded	0	0	0	0	0	0	0	0	0	0	0	0	0
Violating Cuban waters	13	6	3	3	0	0	2	1	0	0	1	0	0
Violating Cuban air space	26	8	17	7	13	3	109	44	4	7	21	10	0
Violating Cuban territory	0	0	2	0	0	0	0	0	1	2	3	46	30
Throwing objects	2	0	3	0	0	0	0	3	2	1	6	1	1
Obscene acts	0	1	5	0	2	0	2	7	0	3	8	1	0
Verbal insults	1	4	14	3	2	2	9	3	0	16	48	4	0

recognizes there may be changes in the conditions under which an agreement was made. In essence, pretending that the Treaty of 1934 is still in effect would be like saying that the reason for its adoption has been behind U.S. policy toward Cuba since 1959—"To strengthen the ties of friendship between the two countries."

The Guantánamo lease is absurd from a legal perspective, and the Treaty of 1934 has lost its reason for being. Consequently, on a legal basis, the base should have been returned to Cuba in 1960. But even if the United States had a legal basis for holding on to the Base at Guantánamo, Cuba's objections are valid since the treaty is obsolete. Cuba's dilemma cannot be reduced to a discussion of international law, though that is important, and in fact supports Cuba. It is a dilemma that has become a central theme in international relations, particularly among Third World nations. Their right to regain sovereignty over their own land and to reject foreign military bases has been upheld by the nations of the Non-Aligned Movement.

As some authors have recognized,[17] the extent to which Cuba has embraced the policies of the Non-Aligned Movement implies that the island nation will reject a foreign military base, demand the return of the Guantánamo Base, and adopt a non-aligned policy of refusing to allow any military bases on Cuban territory. Cuba garners political support for her position from Latin American nations that are part of the Movement, as well as from some nations, such as Mexico, that are not.

At the moment, the base is an infringement of Cuba's sovereignty. If Cuba should repossess the base, it would do so under the principle of sovereignty. Cuba cannot compromise its sovereignty in any agreement or treaty with the United States. Yet, the argument that Guantánamo might become a Soviet base is not supported, either by Cuba's foreign policy, or by the nature of its military collaboration with the USSR. There is no base of this type in Cuba, and no one should logically presume that there will be one in the future. In any case, it would be absurd to think that such a decision might be tied to whether or not Guantánamo were returned.

Final Thoughts

Bilateral agreements between the United States and Cuba emphasize areas of particular interest to both sides—the agreements on highjacking and immigration, for instance. They set an important precedent for possible negotiation on specific points that could be treated separately.

Guantánamo is part of Cuba's national security problem. To resolve this situation, a positive policy must be developed that excludes such hostile acts as piracy, terrorism, and assassination plots against revolutionary leaders. Both sides have recognized that there is some common ground in these matters. Nevertheless, overflights and offshore maneuvers have been a permanent source of irritation for Cuba. During tense periods, such confrontations can have grave consequences. Thus, the solution to the dilemma of the Guantánamo Base could be arrived at through a policy that assures peace and security to both the United States and Cuba. It could be developed in areas such as health and ecology, which haven't yet been explored. Cuba has held out its hand to the United States during one of that country's most hostile periods toward the Revolution since the 1960s. In fact, Cuba only suspended the immigration accord after the United States had taken a unilateral and openly hostile action against Cuba. Against a backdrop of twenty-seven years of instability, and given the ominous character of the United States' formidable military power, the fragile nature of the agreements between the two nations is perfectly understandable.

Cuba might be disposed to negotiate separately the return of the Guantánamo Naval Base. But it is improbable that such a negotiation would be successful in a climate of military threats, or among incidents of piracy, terrorism, and plots to assassinate Cuban leaders. An isolated agreement would likely suffer the same fate as earlier agreements that were not part of an overall understanding. Isolating this issue for the purposes of analysis should not lead us to forget that a stable and definite solution depends on developing a constructive framework for negotiation. For such a framework to exist, the United States must recognize the need to negotiate on an equal footing with Cuba, respecting its sovereignty and its legitimate national security interest.

Reaching a satisfactory agreement on the naval base would bring closer the possibility of such an understanding. It would be an agreement which would concede Cuba's demand for sovereignty, which would be backed by the *force majeure* of international law, and endorsed by the community of nations. The U.S. agreement with Panama over the Panama Canal, ratified within the context of U.S. political and strategic interests, proved that a U.S. decision to negotiate and resolve conflicts over sovereignty can both improve its image abroad and open up new understanding between the two parties.

Notes

1. Principal Report to the First Congress of the Cuban Community Party (CCP) presented by Fidel Castro, DOR, 1975, February 1986, p.224.

2. Reagan backs restraints in relations with Havana (transcript of interview of WRHC Radio Station in Miami, August 27, 1985).

3. There were 4,912 of these violations in 1962, 524 in 1963, and 112 in 1964. In more recent years, there have been fewer—there occurring only 21 such violations in 1983, 10 in 1984, and none in 1985.

4. Castro, Fidel. "Speech at the Conference of the Interparliamentary Union," September 15, 1981, DOR; IV(8), pp.89–111.

5. See Hernández, Rafael. "La Politica de EU hacia Cuba y la cuestion de la migracion." *Cuadernos de Nuestra America,* vol.2, no.3 (January–June, 1985) pp.75–100.

6. See the principal report to the Third Congress of the CCP—the section on "The Revolutionary Armed Forces and the Defense of the Fatherland." (February 1986).

7. Ibid.

8. Hallam, Orval K. "The Need for a New US Policy Toward Cuba in the 1970s." *Naval War College Review,* vol.24, no.7/235 (March 1972), pp.12–13.

9. Ibid., p.13.

10. See Scheina, Martin J. "The US Presence in Guantanamo," in *Strategic Review* (Spring 1976), p.87.

11. Pachter, Henry M. *Collision Course.* New York: Praeger, 1963.

12. See Bonsal, Philip W. *Cuba, Castro and the US.* Pittsburgh, Pennsylvania: University of Pittsburgh Press, p.41; see also Bender, Lynn Darrell. "Las relaciones Cubano-estadounidenses; la prolongacion de hostilidades." Universidad Interamericana, San Juan, Puerto Rico, mimeographed paper, p.11.

13. See Watts, William, and Jorge Dominguez. *The United States and Cuba: Old Issues and New Directions.* Washington, D.C.: Potomac Associates, 1977, p.50.

14. Peterson, Sarah. "A Gulf War for Right to Host the Navy." *US News and World Report* (January 28, 1985), pp.35–36.

15. President Reagan's interview with Soviet journalists, October, 1985.

16. See, among others, Pisani, Miguel A. D'Estefano. *Cuba, Estados Unidos y el derecho internacional contemporaneo.* Editorial Ciencias Sociales, La Habana, 1983; Ministry of Foreign Relations, *Guantánamo, base naval yanqui de crimenes y provocaciones,* Instituto del Libro, La Habana, 1970; Ballart, Gilberto Toste. *La base naval de Estados Unidos en la bahia de Guantanamo,* Editora Politica, La Habana, 1982.

17. See, for example, Chapter One of this book.

7
THE PROBLEM OF
SURVEILLANCE OVERFLIGHTS

7.1 Violations of Cuban Air Sovereignty: The U.S. Reconnaissance Overflights

Jorge Hernández Martinez
Josefina Vidal Ferreiro

Of all the various issues in dispute between Cuba and the United States, the latter's violation of Cuban airspace perhaps best illustrates the asymmetry and the political/strategic focus of the policies with which successive U.S. administrations have confronted the Cuban Revolution. It also demonstrates their hostile nature and disrespect for the rules of diplomacy.

According to the United States, these overflights are supposed to contribute to U.S. security by providing regular inspection of Cuba's offensive capabilities. It is difficult, however, to see how they *do* contribute to that objective. Certainly they represent one of the issues that must be dealt with if the twenty-five-year pattern of hostility is to be changed. Cuba, a small country hard on the flank of the huge United States, has never violated the territorial integrity of the latter; rather, it is Cuba which has often been the object of aggression.

Two primordial needs underlie Cuba's insistence that these violations of her airspace be halted: sovereignty and security. It is our hope that the following observations will suggest ways in which the problem might be constructively approached.

Sovereignty of Cuban Airspace

Though some observers had hoped for an improved atmosphere in U.S.-Cuban relations early in President Reagan's second term, the inauguration of Radio Martí in May of 1985 brought about the exact opposite. Accordingly, Cuba suspended the migration agreement signed the previous year. In spite of the fact that Cuba had sent explicit signals of its willingness to begin a meaningful dialogue and of its disposition to look to the normalization of relations on the basis of mutual respect for one another's sovereignty,[1] the United States chose to maintain its time-worn policy of hostility toward Cuba.[2] It is a policy that substitutes aggression for diplomacy, and that seems to result from a proclivity to see Cuba only as a Soviet satellite—and sometimes almost as a "superpower."

The latter is an important conclusion to bear in mind, for the frequency of U.S. overflights seems to be determined by U.S. perceptions at a given moment of the greater or lesser urgency attached to:

- The offensive character attributed to the Cuban armed forces; and
- The supposed expansionism implicit in the Soviet presence in Cuba.

Not surprisingly, then, the highest levels of violation have coincided with:

- The missile crisis (1962).
- Incidents with respect to an alleged submarine base at Cienfuegos (1970).
- The furor over MiG-23 aircraft (1978).
- The episode of the Soviet "combat" brigade (1979).
- Cuba's supposed involvement in the Central American crisis, and the concomitant increase in Soviet military support for Cuba (1982).

The usefulness of these "reconnaissance" overflights, however, must be questioned. They can hardly be justified on the basis of the aerial photographs thus obtained, for those same photographs could be obtained from U.S. spy satellites. The objective thus seems to be more of a political nature, that is, a show of force, supposedly with the purpose of dissuading the Cuban "superpower" from some act of aggression in the Hemisphere or against the United States. But is this a realistic view? More dispassionate analysis would suggest that it is not.

Sovereignty of airspace is, moreover, enshrined in international law. "It is the principle of *aer clausus,* which establishes the sovereignty of a state over its airspace, and which is incorporated in many international agreements [including air conventions signed in Paris (1919), Havana (1928), and Chicago (1944), the Geneva Convention of 1958 on territorial and contiguous waters, and in numerous agreements of international organizations and decisions of the international courts]. Each state has over its airspace the same sovereign right of property that it has over its land and maritime territory."[3]

Two more considerations should be added to these principles of international law. They relate to the attempt by the United States to justify its overflights by citing OAS resolutions and articles of the Rio Mutual Defense Pact of 1947. With respect to the first, it should be pointed out that Cuba obviously cannot be bound by the resolutions (in this case, the OAS resolution of October 23, 1962) of an organization from which Cuba has been excluded.[4]

And regarding the second, the legitimacy allegedly conferred on the overflights by Articles 6 and 8 of the Rio Treaty cannot be sustained inasmuch as that would be to ignore Article 10 of the same treaty which condemns any violation of the sovereignty of the countries of this Hemisphere.[5]

Security of Cuban Airspace

U.S. policy against Cuba, after the triumph of the Revolution, included in its vast array of aggressions and threats flights that over a period of approximately five years violated Cuban airspace with brutal frequency. As Raul Roa (then Minister of Foreign Affairs of Cuba) summarized the situation in 1964:

> Until April 20 of this year [1964] CIA U-2 aircraft have flown over Cuban territory 600 times. Between November 22 and December 21, 1962, there were 53 flights. During 1963, 454 such espionage missions. And during the current year, there had been 82 flights as of April 20. Other types of aircraft have violated our air space 44 times from November 22, 1962 until April 19, 1964. In addition, U.S. air and naval units constantly carry on espionage activities near our coasts. P-2 V Neptune aircraft make almost daily incursions over Pinar del Rio, Havana and Matanzas provinces, and AC communications ships, such as the AC-159 "Oxford," are stationed off the coast just north of Havana province. Further, our government's frequent denunciation of the harassment of ships engaged in trade with Cuba by low-flying U.S. military aircraft are widely known.[6]

With greater or less intensity, such violations and practices have continued right up to the present day.

On October 22, 1962, President Kennedy declared that the policy of the United States would be: "To consider any launching of nuclear missiles from Cuba against any nation in the Western Hemisphere as an attack on the part of the Soviet Union against the United States—an attack which would require a response from the United States against the Soviet Union itself."[7]

As is widely known, in making public the decision to quarantine Cuba, President Kennedy referred to the defense of U.S. national security and reserved the right to carry out military flights over Cuba in order to assure that security. This rationale underpins the guidelines that prevailed for more than twenty-five years: Cuba has been ignored as the *subject* of its own security and only considered as an *object* of U.S. security.

Cuba opposed, and will always oppose, the unilateral inspection of one country by another against the latter's will. At the same time, it has consistently indicated that it would *not* oppose a system of mutual verification. A note from the Cuban Foreign Ministry, dated April 24, 1964, for example, pointed out that: "The U.S. Government has always rejected the only solution compatible with our national sovereignty— that of mutual verification. U.S. representatives have insisted, rather, on inspection only of Cuba's soil."

In that same vein, President Fidel Castro declared: "We will permit you to inspect us only if you permit us to inspect Florida. Unilateral inspection, no! Such military incursions (including aerial) constitute an act of war and are only legal if preceded by a declaration of war."

Continued violations of Cuban airspace, nonetheless, have been justified by conservative strategists as necessary to prevent "unstable political situations that might open the way to future Soviet incursions into the Hemisphere." At the same time, these strategists acknowledge that "it is improbable that the Soviets might develop Cuba as an important operations base due to U.S. reaction and to the excessive length of the supply lines that would entail."[8]

Generally speaking, conservative analysts tend to exaggerate the reach and capability of Soviet and Cuban forces in the region.[9] The Cuban Armed Forces should be seen for what they are, and their size and characteristics as functions of the international environment. The more intense the pressures and threats against Cuba from the United States, the greater must be Cuba's defensive response.

U.S. analysts speak of a military build-up in Cuba, and of increases in Soviet military assistance, but the fact is that the Cuban Armed Forces are essentially defensive in nature. Cuba was attacked once, at Giron [the Bay of Pigs] in 1961. More recently, it has been threatened again with direct attack. It has every right and—in view of the threats against it—every reason to build up its defenses.

U.S. analysts have also claimed that the MiG-23's range would enable it to reach the southeastern part of the United States, Central America, and many Caribbean nations.[10]

Other specialists, however, have demonstrated that the above is not true. The round-trip range of a combat-laden MiG-23 is *not* sufficient for it to penetrate the southeastern part of the United States. Even if it were, it is absurd to think it would get through U.S. air defenses. And to all that, one must add the unforeseeable consequences such an attack might well have for the peace of the hemisphere—and of the world.[11] What possible gain could make such madness worthwhile?

According to some U.S. analysts, the Cuban navy also is a threat capable of carrying out offensive actions in the Caribbean Basin.[12] Yet, that navy consists only of coastal patrol and torpedo boats, coastal mine sweepers, two Koni-class frigates, and two Whiskey-class submarines.

Only the latter four vessels have distant-water capability. One can imagine how much of a threat the four might pose in the Caribbean Basin, pitted as they would be against the U.S. navy. One would think that U.S. strategists would find it demeaning to suggest such a thing.

To summarize:

* Cuba has developed its defenses in response to the hostile attitude of the United States.
* Cuba has not used its military capabilities for offensive purposes in the Caribbean Basin or against the United States.
* Cuba has not retaliated for violations of its airspace or for other acts of aggression against it.

In view of the above, it ought to be clear that U.S. reconnaissance overflights have little relative value to the security of the United States. Yet, the only positive steps taken by the United States with respect to violations of Cuban airspace were those taken during the Carter Administration. During the first months of 1977, among other measures aimed at achieving a sort of detente in U.S.-Cuban relations, President Carter ordered the termination of flights over Cuban territory. The suspension lasted less than two years, however. Overflights were resumed near the end of 1978, the United States justifying their resumption on grounds that Soviet MiG-23 aircraft, supposedly capable of carrying nuclear weapons, had appeared in Cuba. A press campaign was mounted to present these aircraft as a threat to the security of the region and as a violation of the 1962 Soviet-U.S. understanding.

The government of Cuba, through President Fidel Castro, pointed out that the aircraft had been in Cuba since 1977, a fact of which the United States must have been aware, and noted that they were totally defensive in nature.[13]

Although the U.S. government eventually acknowledged that the

aft, indeed, were not adapted to the transport of nuclear weapons,
... ident Carter, in his report to Congress in February of 1979, stated
that their presence in Cuba continued to be a "matter of concern."[14]

In the same vein, in 1979, the U.S. government conducted the
famous campaign over the presence in Cuba of a Soviet brigade of
approximately 2,000 to 3,000 men. Diplomats from the United States
and the USSR met several times on the issue. In Congress, Senators
Church and Stone were very active in the discussion of the problem.
Their initiative was immediately seconded by Senators De Concini and
Kassenbaum, who linked the brigade problem to global Soviet-U.S.
relations.[15]

Even though President Carter acknowledged that the presence of a
limited number of Soviet personnel in Cuba was not a threat to the
United States, in October of 1979, he approved—perhaps because it
was an election year and he wanted to appear as a strong president—a
series of measures against Cuba. Among these was the augmentation
of reconnaissance overflights.[16]

With the Reagan administration, violations of Cuban airspace were
continued and an atmosphere of intense hostility toward Cuba was
given free rein.

Diplomacy as a Solution

If U.S.-Cuban relations are to be placed on a more sensible, mutually
beneficial plane, the present U.S. policy of force must be replaced by
one of diplomacy—a diplomacy which involves both parties equally on
the basis of mutual respect. The United States must recognize that the
whole context of Inter-American relations has changed, and that within
that new context, Cuba is solidly established as a socialist and non-
aligned country. Once the United States decides to accept that as a
hard fact and to deal with Cuba on a pragmatic basis, the cancellation
of overflights—whose only relative usefulness has been to emphasize
U.S. bad faith toward a small country—would have a most positive
impact. The obliteration of this symbol of arrogance and force might
open the way to the discussion of other problems between the two
countries. It is a step which might be taken for essentially moral
reasons, but which could have practical consequences. Certainly it
would help create a more appropriate climate for negotiations. The
United States would enhance its image by showing respect for a small
country and Cuba would lose a pretext for accusing the United States
of violating international law. Reducing tensions with Cuba would also
help the United States forge a better relationship with the other Latin

American countries, for, as noted by Professor Riordan Roett, "increasing U.S. hostility toward Cuba has become a matter of concern to regional neighbors such as Mexico and Colombia."[17]

Roett also points out that as U.S. policy toward Cuba has failed to achieve its objectives (in other words, has not destabilized or overthrown the Cuban government), it simply gives the impression of U.S. impotence.[18]

For all these reasons, the United States would do well to adopt a more pragmatic and realistic approach to U.S.-Cuban relations. U.S. scholars could contribute to this process by providing objective analysis to correct the present tendency in the United States to exaggerate both the Soviet presence in Cuba and the offensive capabilities of the Cuban Armed Forces.

Finally, it should be borne in mind that the continuation or suspension of these violations of Cuban airspace are taken as a clear indication of a U.S. administration's will to move toward improved relations. Their suspension during the Carter administration was taken as a positive signal; their continuation under Reagan as an impediment to discussions. And what of the future?

Notes

1. See the interviews given by President Fidel Castro to *Excelsior,* March 2, 1985, and to the Spanish News Agency (EFE), February 13, 1985.

2. See, for example, Smith, Wayne S. "Castro Calling," in *The Nation,* February 23, 1985, p.197; and "Cuba: Time for a Thaw," in *The New York Times Magazine,* July 29, 1984, pp.54–56.

3. E'Estefano, Miguel A. *Cuba, Estados Unidos y el Derecho Internacional Contemporaneo.* Havana: Editorial Ciencias Sociales, 1983, pp.134–135.

4. The Symms Amendment would suggest that Cuba is so bound. See *The Congressional Record,* (Senate) 97th Congress, 2nd Session, vol.128, no.20 (March 4, 1982), p.S1660–1662.

5. Article 6. "If the inviolability or the integrity of the territory or sovereignty or political independence of any American state should be affected by an aggression which is not an armed attack or by an intra-continental or extra-continental conflict, or by any other fact or situation that might endanger the peace of America, the organ of consultation shall meet immediately in order to agree on the measures which must be taken in case of aggression to assist the victim of the aggression or, in any case, the measures which should be taken for the common defense and for the maintenance of the peace and security of the continent."

Article 8. "The measures on which the organ of consultation may agree will comprise one or more of the following: Recall of chiefs of diplomatic missions, breaking of diplomatic relations, breaking of consular relations, complete or partial interruption of economic relations or of rail, sea, air, postal, telegraphic, telephonic, radio-telephonic communications, and the use of armed force."

6. Note of April 24, 1964 from the Ministry of Foreign Relations of Cuba; see "Revista Politica Internacional." Havana: MINREX, Instituto de Politica Internacional (May-June 1964), no.6.

7. Cited by Rodman, Peter W. "The Missiles of October: Twenty Years Later." in *Commentary*, vol.74, no.4 (October 1982).

8. Hayes, Margaret Daly. "Dimensionses de seguridad de los intereses de Estados Unidos en America Latina." *International Security*, vol.5, no.1 (Summer 1980), Center for Sciences and International Affairs, Harvard University.

9. See Whalen, Christopher. "The Soviet Military Buildup in Cuba." *The Heritage Foundation Backgrounder*, no.89 (June 11, 1982); and "The Soviet-Cuban Connection in Central America and the Caribbean." Released by the Department of State and Department of Defense, March 1985, Washington, D.C.

10. Thomas, David. "Cuba's Military Machine." *Miami Herald* (April 29, 1984).

11. Cavalla, Antonio, and Ricardo Cordova. "Las Fuerzas de Despliegue Rapido: Nueva guerra de los EEUU en el Tercer Mundo?" Santiago, Chile: *Andes*, no.2 (March 1985), p.89.

12. Thomas, "Cuba's Military Machine."

13. Text of President Fidel Castro's press conference, in *Granma* (November 11, 1978).

14. See Franklin, Jane. *Cuban Foreign Relations: A Chronology, 1959–1982.* New York: Center for Cuban Studies, 1984.

15. These senators were the first to announce evidence of the brigade at the end of July and in August of 1979, and they asked that the issue of ratifying the SALT II treaty be conditioned upon the withdrawal of Soviet troops from Cuba. See: Department of State *Bulletin*, Washington, D.C., Government Printing Office, no.2031, October 1979, pp.14–17.

16. Carter, James E. *Keeping Faith: Memoirs of a President.* New York: Bantam Books, 1983.

17. Roett, Riordan. "La politica exterior de Cuba y los Estados Unidos." In *Cuba-Estados Unidos: Dos Enfoques*, edited by Juan Tokatlian, Bogota: CEREC, 1984.

18. Ibid.

7.2 U.S. Surveillance Overflights _____

Wayne S. Smith
John Buchanan

Ever since the 1962 Missile Crisis, the United States has regularly conducted surveillance overflights of Cuban territory, first with the famous U-2 aircraft and more recently with SR-71s. Only for a brief period during the Carter administration were such overflights halted altogether.

Cuba of course regards these overflights as a violation of her territorial integrity. The United States, on the other hand, considers them necessary to protect its security. It notes that under the Kennedy-Khrushchev understanding of 1962, all offensive weapons systems were to be withdrawn from Cuba and were not to be reintroduced. It notes further that the understanding spoke of the "establishment of adequate arrangements through the United Nations to ensure the carrying out and *continuation of these commitments*."[1] But as Cuba never permitted the U.N. to make such arrangements, the United States has, since 1962, conducted overflights *en lieu* thereof, that is, in order to satisfy itself that no missiles or other nuclear weapons were reintroduced.

With a relaxation of tensions between the two countries, however, the United States could afford to do without the overflights. For one thing, the state of the art today cannot be compared to what it was in 1962. Cameras can now provide pictures from 100 miles up that even low-flying aircraft could not capture twenty-five years ago. Peripheral photography has also improved tremendously, and of course, electronic surveillance now provides a dimension that was virtually unknown in 1962. In short, the United States has the means to get most of the intelligence it needs regarding the importation of weapons systems without overflights.

In 1977, during a brief period of eased tensions, the Carter administration did halt the overflights. It had no reason to believe the Soviet Union might intend to reintroduce offensive weapons systems, or that Cuba would welcome them. Hence, peripheral and satellite photography were deemed adequate to the task at hand. Suspicions were rekindled, however, with the introduction in 1978 of MiG-23 aircraft. The president's military advisors argued that, in light of this new situation, the president must use all means at his disposal, including overflights, to assure against the reintroduction of offensive weapons systems. Their arguments notwithstanding, whether the resumption of overflights was really necessary remains a hotly debated issue—given the fact that other techniques were available. What is not arguable, however, is that renewed tensions led to increased domestic political pressures on the president. In any event, overflights were resumed, and because since 1978 neither tensions nor consequent domestic political pressures have ever abated, the overflights continue.

Under changed circumstances, however, the United States might again feel that it could safely dispense with them. This would require a more relaxed atmosphere. In bringing about such an atmosphere, assurances at a given moment from both the Cuban and Soviet sides that they intend fully to respect the 1962 Kennedy-Khrushchev understanding could be most helpful. It might be useful, indeed, for all three sides, including the United States, to reiterate adherence to the Understanding early in the process of improving relations.

Meanwhile, though the overflights will of course continue to offend Cuba's sense of sovereignty, Cuba can at least console itself with the thought that neither the U-2 nor the SR-71 had, or have, the capability to strike Cuba. They carry no weapons and do not threaten Cuba's security or its people. Further, the flights are conducted at such an altitude that they do not interfere with normal air traffic or safety. Indeed, they are so high that they are on the edge of space and ought not to be appreciably more worrisome to the Cubans than are the satellites which frequently pass over their island.

There is one way in which overflights might be ended even without any significant easing of tensions between the two countries. The 1962 understanding mentioned "adequate arrangements through the United Nations to ensure the . . . continuation of these commitments," that is, United Nations verification that no offensive weapons systems were reintroduced. Were Cuba now willing to discuss the establishment of such U.N. "arrangements," the United States might be in a position to dispense with overflights immediately.

Notes

These remarks deal only with the question of surveillance overflights; violations of Cuban airspace, committed by planes from, or planes conducting operations at, the Guantánamo Naval Base, represent an entirely different problem, which is dealt with in Chapter 6.

   1. From the text of President Kennedy's message of October 27, 1962, to Chairman Khrushchev.

8
THE PROBLEM OF
RADIO INTERFERENCE

8.1 The U.S. View of Radio Interference

John Spicer Nichols

A simple law of physics—that two equidistant radio transmitters broadcasting on the same frequency with equal power will drown each other out—dictates that neighboring nations carefully coordinate their broadcasting systems. Unless the power, frequencies, direction, and times of broadcasting for all radio stations are meticulously controlled, the airwaves can become an indecipherable jumble of competing signals.

If one nation allows its broadcasting stations to encroach on the frequencies allotted to another nation or otherwise disrupt a neighbor's broadcasters, other nations will not feel obligated to protect the offending nation's frequencies. As a result, the finely tuned system breaks down, and the usefulness of the airwaves for all people and nations is severely diminished.

However, in broadcasting's version of "mutual assured destruction," there are no superpowers. The radio transmitters of a small, poor country can be no less disruptive than those of a military or economic superpower. Consequently, neighboring nation—seven unfriendly ones—usually seek accommodation on their use of the radio spectrum.

Nevertheless, radio interference between Cuba and the United States is a long-standing problem that has grown significantly worse in recent years. In the late 1970s, U.S. commercial broadcasters reported increased interference from Cuban transmitters. In 1981, the Reagan administration proposed establishing Radio Martí, only the most recent in a long series of U.S. propaganda stations directed at Cuba since the Bay of Pigs invasion. Radio Martí was approved by the U.S. Congress, after a long and contentious debate, and was inaugurated in 1985. The Cuban government immediately retaliated for the start-up of Radio

Martí by suspending a bilateral immigration agreement, and relations between the two countries quickly deteriorated to their lowest point in recent times.

Although its direct response to Radio Martí was not in the area of broadcasting, the Cuban government announced in 1986 that, during the next five years, it would double the amount it had invested in radio and television since 1959.[1] In the absence of a current radio broadcasting agreement between Cuba and the United States, this massive Cuban expansion would wreak havoc with the U.S. broadcasting system and further contribute to the tensions between the two countries.

Both Cuba and the United States suffer from each other's radio interference; hence, it is in their common interest to solve the problem. When treated as a purely technical matter, Cuban-U.S. radio interference could be rather easily resolved, or at least alleviated. But, when intertwined with larger political and economic disputes, the radio interference problem becomes extraordinarily complex. On the one hand, a radio broadcasting agreement cannot be reached in the hostile, political climate prevailing in U.S.-Cuban relations. On the other hand, progress toward solving technical problems that aggravate both sides could enhance the possibilities of improving overall political relations.

The following discussion identifies the economic, political, and technical incompatibilities between the Cuban and U.S. broadcasting systems and assesses the options for resolving them.

Economic Incompatibilities

The primary battleground between U.S. and Cuban broadcasters is the medium-frequency band, which currently consists of 107 channels from 535 Khz to 1605 Khz on a standard AM radio dial. It is essentially an unexpanding pie from which the United States has long had the lion's share. In recent years, Cuba has attempted to gain a larger share of the regional airwaves, but because a large increase in Cuba's allotment of frequencies probably would mean a loss in frequencies to U.S. broadcasters, the U.S. government has blocked such efforts. Both Cuba and the United States were signatories to the North American Regional Broadcasting Agreements (NARBA), a 1950 multilateral accord that established power limits and maximum levels of interference and provided for the use of directional antennas by high-power stations operating near border areas. Under the agreement, the United States was granted twenty-four unduplicated clear channels and nineteen shared clear channels; Canada received six unduplicated and four shared clear channels; Mexico seven and five; Cuba one and one; and the Bahamas one and zero.[2]

Despite Cuba's long-standing desire to correct these inequities, radio interference was not a significant problem during the first decade of the Revolution. Cut off from replacement parts by the U.S. trade embargo, Cuba was forced to cannibalize its U.S.-built radio stations. During the early 1960s, the number of operating transmitters in Cuba and the aggregate radiated power from those transmitters steadily declined. However, as Cuba established alternative supply lines for radio equipment and began to shift resources into restoration of its antique broadcasting system, the situation changed markedly. By the mid-1970s, Cuba had reversed the decline in number of transmitters and more than doubled their mean power compared to the previous decade. To compound the problem, the new, high-power Cuban stations often did not broadcast on their assigned frequencies, did not use directional antennas and did not reduce their nighttime power to prevent interfering with U.S. stations.[3]

The increased Cuban interference was of particular concern to U.S. commercial broadcasters, whose profits are directly related to the size of their interference-free coverage area. And given the importance of the broadcast media in the U.S. political process, the appeals of the National Association of Broadcasters, the industry lobby, were carefully noted in Washington.

Therefore, by 1981, when Cuba and the United States met in Rio de Janeiro for multilateral negotiations with other Western Hemisphere (Region II) members of the International Telecommunication Union to update frequency allocations, they already were on a collision course. The U.S. government was upset with Cuba's plan to make further large-scale additions to its inventory of medium-wave stations. The Cuban inventory included two 500 Kw transmitters which, if operated at full power, would seriously disrupt U.S. broadcasting.[4] The Cuban government was similarly upset with U.S. resistance to adding new channels to the AM band for Cuban use and with U.S. plans to launch Radio Martí. U.S. diplomats at the Rio meeting ultimately were successful in obtaining a frequency for Radio Martí and in blocking Cuba's attempt to change its station inventory and to win new frequencies. In turn, Cuba withdrew from the meeting without signing the accord and, in 1982, abrogated NARBA.

Political Incompatibilities

Revolutionary Cuba has been the target of the most intense radio propaganda blitz in the history of hemispheric broadcasting. During the 1961 Bay of Pigs invasion, the Central Intelligence Agency operated Radio Swan, a clandestine radio station intended to destabilize the Castro regime. After the failed invasion, Radio Swan was renamed Radio Americas and, until it went off the air in 1968, broadcast shrill, virulent programming urging the Cuban people to sabotage their public utilities, to burn crops, and to rise against the Castro regime.[5] By its very nature, the clandestine station was neither licensed by the U.S. Federal Communications Commission (FCC) nor duly registered with the International Telecommunication Union (ITU), the United Nations body responsible for coordination of the international airwaves. It is also important to note that, prior to the operation of Radio Swan, Cuba generally abided by the NARBA and protected U.S. stations from interference.[6]

During the 1962 Cuban Missile Crisis, the Voice of America (VOA), the official overseas radio service of the U.S. government, began special programming to Cuba from a transmitter on Marathon Key, Florida. The Marathon station was the first to broadcast on medium-wave from the continental United States to a foreign country, in apparent violation of the NARBA and ITU radio regulations (the latter limit medium-wave broadcasting to domestic purposes only).[7] VOA broadcasts to Cuba have been largely replaced by Radio Martí, which technically is a division of Voice of America and broadcasts from the Marathon transmitter. Throughout the 1960s and 1970s, VOA-Marathon and the clandestine Radio Americas were supplemented by a wide variety of other overt and covert stations beamed at Cuba primarily by anti-Castro groups in south Florida. Some of the stations were financed by the CIA; most operated with U.S. government approval or acquiescence.

As the United States lost political and economic leverage over revolutionary Cuba, broadcasting became an important substitute in its foreign policy toward Cuba. In 1980, the so-called Santa Fe Committee, a group of conservative foreign policy analysts which helped to formulate Latin American policy for the Reagan presidential campaign, extended this trend. The committee recommended the creation of Radio Martí, as a major component in a more aggressive stance toward Cuba, suggesting that broadcasting could be used in lieu of military confrontation. However, the committee warned, "If propaganda fails, a war of national liberation against Castro must be launched."[8] In this regard, broadcasting to Cuba is a policy on which most U.S. politicians can agree. A vote for Radio Martí is a highly visible means for congressmen of both political parties to demonstrate inexpensively that they are tough on the Castro regime without resorting to military force.

Consequently, the overarching goal of Cuban broadcasting policy is to counter U.S. intervention via the airwaves. This is largely an extension of Cuba's overall goal of extricating itself from political, economic and cultural dominance by the United States. As such, Cuba maintains that a nation's airwaves are sovereign—a view shared by most communist and Third World nations and supported by a body of international law intended to discourage the use of the airwaves for hostile propaganda and political coercion.[9] In contrast, the United States and many of its Western allies argue for the "free flow" of broadcasting across national boundaries and charge that East bloc jamming of incoming radio signals is a violation of international law. The Western position also has basis in a number of treaties and U.N. resolutions.[10]

Cuba's response to U.S. broadcasts has been both retaliatory and defensive. Cuban counterbroadcasts have been mostly on short-wave (the band designated by ITU for legitimate international broadcasting), but some have been on medium-wave:

- From 1962 to 1965, Cuba broadcast Radio Free Dixie on medium-wave to the United States. The program called on U.S. blacks to commit acts of violence and subversion.
- For four hours during the night of August 30, 1982, The Voice of Cuba broadcast English-language programming on at least six AM channels causing interference to U.S. broadcasters. Cuban officials said that it was a "test and demonstration" of Cuba's ability to respond to Radio Martí. The U.S. station most affected was WHO Radio in Des Moines, Iowa, which formerly was the employer of sportscaster Ronald Reagan and which broadcasts on 1040 Khz, the frequency originally scheduled for use by Radio Martí.
- In 1980 and 1981, Cuba relayed Radio Moscow's English-language service, which was heard on AM over much of the eastern United States. And, during the summer of 1987, Cuban radio began experiments apparently aimed at reviving the Soviet programming to the United States. However, at this writing, Cuba's huge 500 Kw transmitters had not been unleashed at full power, forestalling serious disruption to U.S. broadcasters.

Instead, Cuba has emphasized its defensive strategy. It continued jamming the VOA/Radio Martí frequency, but at a very low level, apparently intended to express its displeasure rather than to block the signal. However, Miami-area commercial stations operated by Cuban exiles are more heavily jammed. For example, Radio Mambí (WAQI), a new Spanish-language station, which boasts that it broadcasts anti-Castro programming to Cuba, is not clearly heard in Havana. More important, Cuba has escalated construction of high-power transmitters intended to fill vacant frequencies and ward off alien radio signals. However, Cuba's attempt to build a protective wall against U.S. radio propaganda is also causing serious interference to innocent U.S. commercial stations.[11]

The U.S. government publicly denies any relationship between Cuban radio interference with U.S. stations and U.S. propaganda broadcasts to Cuba, and it heretofore has been successful in separating the issues at ITU negotiating sessions.[12] However, its position is disingenuous. A 1981 U.S. State Department report, which was declassified and obtained under the Freedom of Information Act, concluded:

> If the decision is made to establish (Radio Martí), we believe Cuba will retaliate by increasing its current level of interference with U.S. AM broadcasting operations. . . . We are meeting at the technical level with Cuba to find solutions for the existing and potential interference problems. Announcement and certainly establishment of (Radio Martí) prior to the completion of the (Rio) broadcasting conference would frustrate resolution of the problems of U.S. broadcasters.[13]

Furthermore, in order to gain support of U.S. broadcasters, congressional sponsors of Radio Martí added a clause to the enabling legislation that provided for federal compensation to commercial stations suffering from Cuban interference. This was tacit admission of a strong linkage between the interference problem and U.S. propaganda to Cuba.

Both Cuba and the United States have been guilty of a double standard in their respective positions on cross-national broadcasting. While arguing that its airwaves are sovereign, Cuba built the largest international broadcasting operation in the Hemisphere which, particularly during the 1960s, aired some highly inflammatory programming to neighboring Latin American countries. However, during secret U.S.-Cuban negotiations in Mexico in 1986, Cuban officials said that they would drop their objections to Radio Martí and restore the immigration agreement, if the United States would grant Cuba equal access to U.S. airwaves. But the U.S. government, the foremost advocate of the "free flow" principle of international broadcasting, rejected the compromise on the grounds that the proposed Cuban broadcasts would badly disrupt U.S. radio stations. Saying, in effect, that what is good for the goose is not necessarily good for the gander, the United States broke off negotiations, and the impasse on the intertwined broadcasting and immigration issues continues.

Technical Incompatibilities

Radio signals are obedient only to the laws of nature and will wander into the assigned coverage areas of other radio stations unless steps are taken to prevent such interference. While both the United States and Cuba attempt to protect their broadcasting systems from harmful interference, the methods they use are markedly different. Given that radio waves do not recognize political boundaries and given the geographic proximity of the two countries, these technical incompatibilities badly exacerbate the radio interference problem.

The U.S. broadcasting system is a sophisticated jigsaw puzzle in which the irregular coverage patterns of some 5,000 radio stations are painstakingly pieced together so that the stations do not seriously interfere with one another. During the daytime hours, when radio waves (known as ground waves) move along the surface of the earth, the distance AM radio signal travels depends primarily on the power of the transmitter. By meticulously regulating the power and other engineering factors, and by requiring most stations to use directional antennas, the Federal Communications Commission maintains order on the U.S. domestic airwaves.

During the nighttime hours, when radio waves (known as sky waves) bounce off the ionosphere, AM signals travel many times farther than during the daytime. Under certain conditions, sky-wave signals can be clearly heard more than a thousand miles away. To prevent nighttime interference, the FCC requires some stations to leave the air and others to reduce their power shortly after sunset. Most interference, especially Cuban interference, occurs at night.

To some extent, interference is always present in a complex broadcasting system; however, interference is usually defined as "objectionable" when it is greater than five percent—that is, when an interfering signal is 1/20th as strong as a station's own signal inside its assigned coverage area one out of ten nights. Five percent interference is barely audible, but 16 percent interference is very annoying to listeners, especially during music programming. In the United States, interference problems normally are solved by reducing power of the offending transmitter.

Because the U.S. broadcasting system is so finely tuned and relies so heavily on sky-wave service, it is particularly vulnerable to disruption. Just one renegade station operating inside the United

States or from a neighboring country at a time or level of power not coordinated under national or international agreements will have a ripple effect throughout the U.S. broadcasting system.[14]

In contrast, Cuba has a much less sophisticated and, therefore, much less vulnerable broadcasting system. The coverage areas of Cuban transmitters frequently overlap, and interference problems are normally solved by increasing power to overcome the competing signal. Cuba does not use nighttime sky-wave service. Instead, it uses small twenty- to thirty-mile ground-wave service areas and repeats the same programming on different frequencies in towns only fifty to sixty miles away.[15] While this Soviet-style system is tremendously wasteful of radiated power and frequencies, it is nearly impregnable to outside radio signals. In fact, there is considerable evidence to suggest that Cuba's development of this type of system is less a product of unsophisticated engineering and more a conscious defensive strategy to protect its radio from foreign intervention. In either case, the Cuban broadcasting system, because of its use of high power, would be far more durable than the U.S. system in the event of an all-out radio war. But even if a radio war is avoided, the interference problem will worsen as long as the United States attempts to broadcast to Cuba. Each time a new U.S. government station (such as Radio Martí) or commercial station sponsored by Cuban exiles (such as Radio Mambí) goes on the air, Cuba fills more frequencies and increases power on existing frequencies which, in turn, causes more interference to innocent U.S. broadcasters.

Options for Resolution of the Radio Interference Problem

1. Unilateral actions by the United States.
   a. The FCC has granted Special Temporary Authority for some U.S. stations to increase their power or change their antennas in order to recover some of their service area lost to Cuban interference. However, this short-term solution to the problem merely contributes to the long-term decline of AM radio service. Given their normal behavior, Cuban broadcasters are likely to match increases in U.S. power, thereby compounding the interference. Furthermore, U.S. broadcasters using STAs usually cannot regain their entire coverage area and probably will cause interference to other U.S. stations. This solution is also costly and risky for U.S. broadcasters. Under FCC rules, the broadcasters must return to their original power and antenna configuration if the interfering Cuban transmitter changes its

frequency or reduces its power.   In sum, STAs treat the symptoms rather than the cause.[16]

b. During the congressional debate over the creation of Radio Martí, State Department officials told nervous commercial broadcasters that the U.S. government was prepared to take "extreme measures" in the event of massive and intentional interference from Cuba.   The measures reportedly included military action against Cuban transmitters and disruption of Cuban communications with the use of highly classified U.S. communications technology.[17]

2. Unilateral technical concessions by Cuba.

a. The most common suggestion by U.S. broadcasters and diplomats for reducing interference is for Cuba to resume using directional antennas.   This would reduce interference to stations in the United States and in friendly, third-party nations as well as to many Cuban stations, but it is contrary to more than a decade of Cuban broadcasting policy and procedures.   Further, there is little motivation for Cuba to undertake these expensive modifications without a *quid pro quo* from the United States and some resolution to the problem of U.S. political broadcasts to Cuba.

b. The best technical solution is for Cuba to expand its FM broadcasting system instead of its AM system.   Because FM is line-of-sight broadcasting in which the radio signals travel only short distances, Cuba could fill as many frequencies with high-power stations as it wished without causing interference to U.S. and its own stations.   Here again, there is little motivation for Cuba to make the expensive switch-over to FM, particularly without a U.S. guarantee of nonintervention on the AM frequencies not filled by Cuban transmitters.

3. Unilateral U.S. political concessions.

a. Cuban officials repeatedly have demanded that the Radio Martí dispute must be resolved before they will negotiate with the United States on immigration, radio interference, or other bilateral issues.   If a future U.S. administration made the strategic decision to improve relations with Cuba, the tactical desirability of political broadcasting would be greatly reduced, and Radio Martí could be terminated or blended back into the regular VOA programming.   However, given the domestic political implications of Radio Martí and the continued hostility between the two nations, this outcome seems highly unlikely in the near future.

Nevertheless, a U.S. administration could take a number of

intermediate, confidence-building, or symbolic actions that might help to end the impasse. For example, the U.S. government could change the name of the station. Cuban officials assert that using the name of Jose Martí, the Cuban national hero, is an unacceptable affront, and their anger over the usurpation of the patriotic symbol seems genuine. Indeed, the U.S. Congress anticipated this symbolic dispute and, in the compromise legislation that created the station, specifically prescribed a less inflammatory name, for example, Voice of America: Cuban Service. Dropping the Radio Martí label would be a painless concession that might allow the United States to keep its radio station, Cuba to keep its pride, and both to resume negotiations on radio interference and other issues.

However, it probably would not be productive for the United States to further explore Cuba's 1986 proposal to end its opposition to Radio Martí if it is allowed to similarly broadcast on U.S. airwaves. The problem with this proposal is that the U.S. frequencies are jam-packed, and licensed U.S. broadcasters would have to be removed from the air to make room for the Cuban station. Such an action would have complex and far-reaching legal implications, and domestic, political constituencies probably would oppose direct Cuban access to U.S. audiences, despite the "free flow of information" ideology of the United States and its practice of that ideology toward Cuban audiences.

b. The U.S. government could be more aggressive in closing down clandestine anti-Castro stations operating in Florida. While these stations are little more than an annoyance to Cuba, taking them off the air would have considerable symbolic value. In the early 1980s, the FCC launched a major campaign to silence the unlicensed clandestines, but following resistance from other sectors of the administration, the effort waned.[18] The FCC also has considerable leeway to impose restraints on Florida commercial stations that broadcast inflammatory programming to Cuba. Although they would be politically unpopular with Cuban exile groups, such actions would not necessarily violate the free speech provisions of the U.S. Constitution. The U.S. Supreme Court has ruled that the federal government's right and responsibility to conduct foreign policy is plenary. Therefore, when a radio station broadcasts to a foreign audience, its First Amendment rights probably do not exceed the government's interest in maintaining international relations. Moreover, the United States is obligated, under international treaties, to prevent hostile propaganda emanating from its territory.[19]

4. Expansion of the AM band: Increasing the number of available AM frequencies for use by Cuba and other countries that feel short-changed from previous allocations would help solve the economic—but not the political—incompatibilities. Both the United States and Cuba initially supported a proposal that would have reduced the spacing between channels from 10 Khz to 9 Khz, thereby increasing the number of slots on the AM band. This change could be accomplished without significant increases in interference, but under pressure from commercial broadcasters unwilling to absorb the costs of the switch-over, the U.S. government changed its position. Cuba cited U.S. efforts to block the 9 Khz proposal as a major reason for the breakdown in negotiations.[20]

In 1986, the Region II nations, including Cuba, met in Geneva and agreed to add 100 Khz of the spectrum to the top of the AM band, making room for hundreds of new stations on ten new channels. Theoretically, some of the expanded band could be used to satiate Cuba's appetite for more frequencies, and perhaps even a clear channel for counter-broadcasting to the United States. The new frequencies should be available by 1990.

5. ITU mediation: The International Telecommunication Union is the United Nations body designated to help nations resolve radio interference problems, but it has been notoriously ineffective when technical issues are intertwined with politics. In 1983, Cuba and the United States held secret talks in Costa Rica under the auspices of the ITU; predictably, they broke down over political issues. Since then, both countries have filed formal complaints with the ITU. But the U.S. government is not likely to rely heavily on the good offices of the ITU for further negotiations, given the administration's current attitude toward the World Court, UNESCO, and other U.N. bodies.

Conclusion

The key questions in resolving this dispute are: At what point are the economic and technical costs so great that the United States will forgo the domestic and international political benefits of broadcasting to Cuba? And if the United States were to end or reduce its political broadcasts, would Cuba undertake expensive and complex alterations in its broadcasting system as a price for reduced tension in the region?

The status quo benefits neither side, and each time Cuba or the

United States turns up the power of an existing transmitter or commits a new one to the radio propaganda and interference battle, resources are wasted and AM radio service for listeners on both sides of the Straits of Florida deteriorates further. The two countries reached this predicament after twenty-five years of step-by-step escalations on the airwaves (see Appendix), but very little room for additional escalations remains without serious disruption. Only a modicum of restraint on both sides has prevented a total breakdown in the regional broadcasting system.

At a time when both countries are poised for further escalation in their broadcasting confrontation, means of reversing the cycle and beginning a step-by-step de-escalation should be urgently explored. As Kalmann Schaefer, longtime FCC expert on international communications and chair of the U.S. delegation at the Rio negotiations, told a congressional committee, "The choice is stark: Mutual accommodation or chaos."[21]

Notes

The author gratefully acknowledges: The Pennsylvania State University and Palmer Communications, Inc., for their financial support of field research in Cuba; Kenneth D. Salomon, an attorney representing Palmer, for sharing documents he obtained under the Freedom of Information Act; and Sydney W. Head of the University of Miami for his comments on an earlier draft of this manuscript.

1. "Notable funding for Cuban radio and TV." *Granma Weekly Review* (March 2, 1986), p. 3.

2. Head, Sydney W. *Broadcasting in America: A Survey of Television and Radio,* 3rd ed. Boston: Houghton Mifflin Company, 1976, p. 41. Also see Frederick, Howard H. *Ideology in International Telecommunication: Radio Wars between Cuba and the United States,* Ph.D. dissertation, American University, 1979; and Antich, Arnaldo Coro. *La guerra radial de Estados Unidos contra Cuba.* Habana: Universidad de La Habana, 1985. Clear channels are the most prized, on the radio spectrum, because stations broadcasting on them may use maximum power during the nighttime hours, allowing their signals to travel many hundreds of miles.

3. Schatz, Ronald F. "Formal Comments," unpublished paper submitted to the Federal Communications Commission, April 4, 1983, part 2. P. 48; Federal Communications Commission, "Cuban MF Broadcasting Interference, United States Government, April 1986." Unpublished press kit. Schatz notes that Cuban compliance with frequency assignments greatly increased in 1980, when it reorganized its AM inventory, and 1982. This implies that Cuban interference is more the result of technical problems associated with the reorganization of its broadcast system than a deliberate attempt to interfere with U.S. stations.

4. Maximum operating power for clear channel stations in the United

States is 50 Kw, one-tenth the power of the two Cuban transmitters.

5. Soley, Lawrence C., and John S. Nichols, *Clandestine Radio Broadcasting.* New York: Praeger Publishers, Inc., 1987.

6. Schatz, Ronald F. "Cuban M.W. Broadcasting in Perspective." Unpublished paper, 1982; *Radio Broadcasting to Cuba,* hearing before the Committee on Foreign Relations, U.S. Senate, 97 Cong. 2 Sess., Pt. II. Washington: U.S. Government Printing Office, 1983, p. 68. While it appears that, for political reasons, the United States was the first to violate NARBA, there is no guarantee that Cuba would not have eventually violated NARBA for the economic reason cited in the previous section.

7. VDA-Marathon also operated without a FCC license. ITU radio regulations prohibit medium-wave stations from purposely broadcasting across national boundaries. If broadcasters wish to reach foreign audiences, they are expected to use short-wave. *Radio Broadcasting to Cuba,* p. 84.

8. *Radio Broadcasting to Cuba,* pt. 1, p. 14.

9. Whitton, John B., and Arthur Larson. *Propaganda: Towards Disarmament in the War of Words.* Dobbs Ferry, NY: Oceana Publications, 1963.

10. Head, Sydney W. *World Broadcasting Systems.* Belmont, CA: Wadsworth Publishing Company, 1985, chapters 11 and 12; Read, William H. "International Radio Broadcasting: Sovereignty Versus Free Flow." In *Toward a Law of Global Communications Networks,* edited by Anne W. Branscomb. New York: Longman Inc., 1985.

11. Cornette, Mary Low. *Cuban Interference with Commercial United States Amplitude Modulated Radio Stations,* M.A. thesis, Colorado State University, 1984; Ducey, Richard V. "U.S. Broadcast Industry Concerns About Radio Broadcasting To Cuba and Potential Cuban Responses: The Case of Radio Martí." Paper presented to Telecommunications Policy Research Conference, Airlie, Virginia, April 1986.

12. U.S. Department of State. "Radio Martí and Cuban Interference." Current Policy No. 392, Washington, D.C., May 10, 1982; *Radio Broadcasting to Cuba,* pp. 72–75.

13. U.S. Department of State. "Impact on Domestic AM Broadcasting." Confidential document, n.d.

14. Rau, Michael C. "Cuban Interference to United States Broadcasting." Unpublished report by the National Association of Broadcasters, n.d.

15. *Radio Broadcasting to Cuba,* Pt. 2, p. 44; Schatz, "Comments," Pt. 1, pp.2–4.

16. Schatz, "Comments," Pt. 1, p. 9.

17. Holsendolph, Ernest. "U.S. Lists 'Options' on Cuban Jamming." *The New York Times* (May 5, 1983), p. 5.

18. Soley and Nichols, *Clandestine Radio Broadcasting,* chap. 7.

19. Uttaro, Ralph A. "The Voices of America in International Radio Propaganda." *Law and Contemporary Problems,* Duke University School of Law, v. 45 (Winter 1982), p. 119; Whitton and Larson, *Propaganda,* pp. 104–133; Martin, Jr., John. *International Propaganda: Its Legal and Diplomatic Control.* Minneapolis: University of Minnesota Press, 1958.

20. Subcommittee on International Operations of the Committee on Foreign Affairs, U.S. House of Representatives, *Region 2 Administrative Radio Conference on Medium Wave Frequency (MF) Broadcasting,* Hearings, 97th Cong., 1st Sess. (Washington: Operations, *Oversight of Region 2 Administrative Radio Conference on Medium Wave Frequency Broadcasting,* Hearings, 97th Cong., of Representatives, *Radio Broadcasting to Cuba (Radio Martí),* Hearing and Markup, 97th Cong., 2nd Sess. (1982).

21. *Radio Broadcasting to Cuba,* Pt. 1, p. 171.

8.2 Radio Interference:
A Cuban View _____

_____ Arnaldo Coro Antich

When the Cuban Revolution swept to victory in 1959, the Cuban broadcast system had only two 50 kilowatt radio stations, some 10 Kw transmitters in the capital and a few in other cities. The rest of the country's radio equipment was made up of 5 Kw, 1 Kw, and 500 watt transmitters. It should be pointed out that the low-powered transmitters found in local stations were almost always connected to inefficient antennas installed on the roofs of buildings, and had such weak signals that they rarely affected the broadcasts in other countries.

This broadcast "system," except for the Education Ministry's CMZ Radio, was completely commercial. Its primary objective was not to serve the citizens of the country, but rather, to transmit only to those areas where the population had buying power that would make it profitable for the owner of the station to sell advertising.

The following fact might be illuminating. The most powerful radio equipment outside of Havana was operated by the CMQ Circuit, S. A. in Santa Clara. A 15 Kw transmitter, it nevertheless used a directional antenna with two towers to protect the distant threat of Station KFI's 500 microvolts. The 640 Khz KFI station is located in Los Angeles, California.

The revolutionary government immediately began operating the various stations that had belonged to the tyrant, Fulgencio Batista, and to his figureheads and collaborators. This was the nucleus from which developed Cuba's National Broadcasting System, whose basic objective from the beginning was to serve the country's whole population. In 1959, the Telecommunications Advisory Committee, and later, in 1960, the Bureau of Broadcast Coordination, both of them branches of the Communications Ministry, conducted research studies and supported projects that would provide Cuba with the minimum in essential radio services.

It was in 1960 that the United States began taking aggressive action against Cuba in the field of broadcasting. These actions paralleled the military plans the United States organized through its Central Intelligence Agency, or CIA.

These aggressive actions took several forms. In this chapter, however, we will limit ourselves to pointing out those actions carried out on the medium-wave band between 535 and 1605 Khz.

Let us examine some significant examples that illustrate the different aggressive tactics the United States has taken.

The Clandestine, or Pirate Station, Radio Swan: The creation of the CIA's propaganda expert, David Atlee Phillips, Radio Swan, broadcast at 1160 Khz, a channel assigned by NARBA to Station KSL in Salt Lake City, Utah. Radio Swan's signals covered almost all of Cuba's territory, gaining particular intensity at night and blotting out the 1160 Khz frequency in Cuba. A directional antenna was installed on Swan Island to lessen interference with the transmissions of Station KSL in Utah, especially during the station's evening broadcasts. Nevertheless, the owners of KSL complained often, until they were silenced by U.S. government officials who told them the transmissions were of "special interest to the White House."

WMIE Miami, the 1950's Version of a Station that was Registered with NARBA: This transmitter operated at 1140 Khz and was set up to broadcast in Spanish to Cuba. The station had the added advantage of a directional antenna that was designed to protect it from stations to the north. Thus the WMIE antenna could transmit undesirable broadcasts to Cuba, producing an intense signal, particularly in the central area of the island.

Just as it did in Miami on WGBS, 710 Khz, the United States fought aggressively on the airwaves, defending its actions with citations from the North American Broadcasting Agreement, which the United States had itself drawn up, in 1950, in Washington, D.C.

Congressman Pucinski's so-called Committee for Democracy served as a way to finance the radio transmissions to Cuba from the United States, both through short-wave and medium-wave bands.

To cite a few examples, destabilizing and subversive programs were transmitted from Miami, from Key West (WKWF, 1600 Khz), from New Orleans, Louisiana (WLW, 870 Khz), and at a given moment, from Charlotte, North Carolina (WBT, 1110 Khz).

The period from 1960 to 1962 was characterized by an increase in both the number of broadcasts and in stations that broadcast on medium-wave to Cuba from the United States.

But in 1962, during the October Crisis, the United States launched against Cuba an unprecedented wave of radio propaganda in which medium-wave radio stations played a fundamental role. First, the Voice of America broadcast was "voluntarily" re-transmitted by a great number of U.S. radio stations, whose signals, thanks to NARBA, were heard in Cuba in all their intensity. Second, the U.S. navy installed, with great speed, two mobile 50 Kw transmitters, each equipped with a directional antenna turned toward Cuba. In direct violation of NARBA, the U.S. government chose to broadcast at 1040 and 1180 Khz. The 1040 Khz station was located in Sugar Loaf Key and the other at Marathon. So the United States reached a new stage in its radio-driven hostilities against Cuba. And the actions continued beyond the crisis, as the two medium-wave transmitters stayed on the air with Voice of America's Spanish language programming for Latin America. One segment of that programming was called "Rendezvous with Cuba," which could be considered the forerunner of Radio Martí.

It is interesting to note the absolute and total illegality of these medium-wave transmissions from the Florida Keys, which we can prove with a look at the Frequency Registry of the International Board of the Union of International Telecommunications. Nowhere in the organization's archives is there proof that the U.S. administration reported to the International Frequency Registration Board (IFRB), a specialized branch of the International Telecommunications Union, the radio installations operating from the Florida Keys.

In the preparatory stages of the Medium-Wave Regional Administrative Conference, held in Rio de Janeiro in 1981, the U.S. delegation admitted the illegal status of the Marathon transmitter. At the time, the station had been failing for nineteen years to comply with the Ruling on Radiocommunications, which was established and approved in 1973 by the signers to the International Telecommunications Convention held in Málaga-Torremolinos, Spain.

The Sugar Loaf Station was destroyed by a hurricane in 1966. It was not re-built until 1982, when the U.S. navy again installed a 50 kilowatt transmitter, this time at Saddle Bench Key. The new antenna was a four-tower, directional array and transmitted at 1040 Khz. A brief test period of the navy's 1040 Khz transmitter was heard in July of 1982. The renovated system was submitted to tests in July 1982. According to what the FCC informed the IFRB, the transmitter's directional antenna was pointed toward Cuba.

The choice of the 1040 Khz frequency seems to have been made by the National Telecommunications Administration, based on studies of the status of the radio spectrum in the area. The Saddle Bench station was the object of a debate in Congress because it was built by the Secretary of Defense, with secret funds, and without congressional approval. This was the original station from which Radio Martí was to broadcast, because under the plans of the Reagan Administration, the Voice of America repeater in Marathon was going to be kept on the air at 1180 Khz with a 50 Kw transmitter.

In the period being analyzed here, it is evident that the U.S. government created the conditions that allowed medium-wave radio transmissions to Cuba from U.S. territory, and that, in so doing, it violated both international law and its own laws.

Following a long debate in Congress, that lasted from 1981 to October 4, 1983, a new law was approved that gave birth to a new era in radio transmissions to Cuba.

Public Law 98-111 represented a compromise solution hammered out in order to obtain agreement from U.S. legislators who were opposed to the original idea of the station. Finally, they succeeded in creating an agency that would be subordinate to the Voice of America, but would be relatively independent of it. The Reagan Administration wanted the new broadcasting entity, which was named Radio Martí, to become part of the Board for International Broadcasting, a semi-autonomous agency that comprises Radio Free Europe and Radio Liberty. But the administration accepted the Voice of America option in order to gain approval from Congress.

From the first days of October 1983 until May 20, 1985, preparations were made, and personnel hired, for the day when the station would go on the air.

Initially, the idea was to transmit at 1180 Khz from Marathon, superseding that station's broadcast of the Voice of America's Latin American programming. At the same time, high-powered, short-wave radio transmitters in Bethany, Ohio, and Greenville, North Carolina, would direct the new station's signals toward Cuba. In this initial scheme, the programming would be scheduled between 5:30 a.m. and 1:30 p.m., and between 4:30 p.m. and 11 p.m. Several months later, the hours of operation were increased, and by February 10, 1986, the programming was running seventeen and a half hours a day. We believe it is proper to note that Radio Martí is not the only station whose signals are directed toward Cuba with both the approval and financial backing of the U.S. government.

The most recent example of this is the installation of a new station in Miami, WAQI, 710 Khz, whose signals are also directed toward Cuba. Radio Mambí went on the air October 23, 1985, with an aggressive speech given by Armando Perez Roura, a counter-revolutionary of Cuban origin.

We should point out that this station was the former WGBS, which was used against Cuba in the 1960s. It was sold, with the approval of the FCC, to a group of people whose obvious intentions were to transmit programs to Cuba, given the station's high-powered 50,000 watt system and a directional antenna pointed at our country.

This step made it obvious that the most recalcitrant anti-Cuban circles were not satisfied with the compromise that made Law 98-111 possible. They wanted the broadcasts that they had conceived, and that would be even more aggressive, as can be seen in a preliminary analysis of the WAQI broadcasts.

The Reagan administration's approval of Radio Mambí marked the beginning of a new era in the use of medium-wave radio stations against Cuba, and only a few months after Radio Martí went on the air.

The Current Situation

As I write these lines, the medium-wave broadcast systems in the United States and Cuba operate with no understanding, modus vivendi, or regulatory agreement. This situation produces problems in the radio broadcasts of both countries, during the day, and at night.

According to the records of the IFRB, which were reviewed at the Regional Conference on Broadcasting in 1981, Cuba had originally planned to use 106 of the 107 channels in the medium-wave range.

Daytime interference is more limited because the signals are transmitted on the so-called ground wave. At night, however, a great deal of interference occurs, which affects the broadcasts of countless stations in both countries.

The absence of a realistic technical arrangement that could establish an operating standard for radio stations, makes it a complex and difficult proposal to operate systems in both countries. The FCC has allowed a number of Special Temporary Authority classifications, or STA, which permit a number of U.S. stations to increase the power of their broadcasts aimed at Cuba.

If no agreement exists, how can the United States explain the legal basis for qualifying as "jamming" the interference between U.S. and Cuban broadcasts?

It is obvious that the United States is not limiting itself to the establishment of radio stations whose Spanish-language programming is aimed at Cuba. The United States is also calling for the right to classify as "jamming" the signals from Cuban stations that reach the United States in the normal course of Cuba's broadcasting schedule.

What interest, for example, does Cuba have in transmitting broadcasts from a provincial station, in Sancti Spiritus, to the suburbs of Philadelphia? Until a few years ago, the Providence of Sancti Spiritus had huge areas that had never been reached by a radio signal. It wasn't until the end of the 1960s that Cuba had the resources to provide this vital service to the local population. The frequency was carefully chosen to provide the best service possible, but it was inevitable that, during the evening hours, the new station would generate interference with U.S. stations that occupy the same channel.

Without doubt, the operation of U.S. and Cuban radio stations could be made more compatible by using the internationally acceptable means described in this paper. The process of searching for and implementing such a solution must be based on mutual respect, absolute reciprocity, and fairness, and could bring about a reduction of incompatibilities in some cases, and an end to them in others.

Is it possible that someday the medium-wave radio broadcast systems of Cuba and the United States could operate with the minimum level of interference?

Is it possible that the broadcast systems of both countries could be made compatible during both day and night? Why not? It only requires that both governments commit themselves to the achievement of such a situation. The United States has always declared that it subscribes to a Free Flow of Information. Yet, in the case of medium-wave broadcasts, from 1960 until recently—and most notably with the establishment of Radio Martí in 1985—it had in practice allowed a flow in only one direction. Its medium-wave broadcasts were beamed at Cuba and could be heard throughout the island. Cuban broadcasts had not had similar access to U.S. airwaves. Apparently this is about to change. In November of 1987, U.S. negotiators agreed to try to work out means of giving Cuba some degree of access to medium-wave broadcasting for coverage of U.S. territory. How successful these efforts will be remains to be seen, but the fact that they are to be made at all is encouraging. Optimistically, it suggests a changing attitude on the part of the United Statesa change toward a more reciprocal and symmetrical approach to the radio problem. Let us hope this portends an atmosphere in which the problem could be fully addressed and put behind us. The advantages would be many: better service with fewer material and energy resources needed by either side.

As established by the International Agreement on Telecommunications, national governments exert sovereignty over their respective communications systems and are thus empowered to take steps to reduce interference between or among broadcasting systems.

To this end, it is standard practice to arrange agreements, or modus vivendi statutes that define the operational parameters of the stations that the parties wish to make compatible. It would consequently be reasonable to begin sometime in the future a process of bilateral talks and preliminary negotiations between the United States and Cuba that could lead to an agreement on the legal norms for the eventual signing of such a document.

8.3 Appendix: Chronology of Events Related to U.S.-Cuban Radio Interference ⎯⎯⎯⎯⎯⎯⎯⎯⎯⎯⎯

January 1, 1959. Fidel Castro came to power in Cuba.

February 23, 1960. U.S. Senate ratified the North American Regional Broadcasting agreements (NARBA), which had been negotiated by the United States, Cuba, Canada, the Bahamas, Jamaica, the Dominican Republic, and Haiti in 1950 and updated in 1958. The vast majority of the clear-channel frequencies and total frequencies were allotted to the United States. The agreements also established technical standards to resolve AM radio interference problems in the region and replaced the first NARBA, signed in 1937 and updated in 1946.

March 17, 1960. President Eisenhower approved a covert action plan against Cuba, including the use of a "powerful propaganda campaign."

March 21, 1960. Voice of America (VOA), the official U.S. government overseas broadcast service, resumed Spanish-language programming "edited with an eye toward Cuba."

March 23, 1960. Classified memo to the U.S. Secretary of State (released under the Freedom of Information Act) reviewed stepped-up VOA broadcasts to Cuba on short wave. The memo also discussed other possible U.S. Information Agency (USIA) activities directed at Cuba, including the use of the USS Courier (a communications ship which broadcast on short-wave and medium-wave), a broadcasting airplane, or a new medium-wave transmitter mounted at Key West, but it recommended "holding off" because those acts would "leave the United States open to charges of increased psychological warfare against Cuba."

March 31, 1960. U.S. Congressman Paul G. Rogers of Florida called a confidential meeting of officials of the State Department, Federal Communications Commission (FCC), and VOA to discuss the willingness of six commercial radio stations in southern Florida to broadcast Spanish-language programming to Cuba. The congressman noted, however, that the stations were prohibited from increasing their power because of the NARBA treaty with Cuba. The FCC and VOA representatives explained the technical reasons for the agreement with Cuba and warned that "the United States would suffer considerably from any radio war with Cuba." The State Department's declassified minutes of the meeting (obtained under the Freedom of Information Act) also noted, without explanation, that "the Castro Government has approached certain broadcasting companies in Florida with the view of buying radio time."

May 17, 1960. Radio Swan, an anti-Castro station created by the U.S. Central Intelligence Agency (CIA) in response to the Eisenhower-approved plan for covert operations against Cuba, went on the air. The transmitters, broadcasting on both short-wave and medium-wave, were on U.S.-claimed Swan Island in the Caribbean, and the programming was produced in Miami by the CIA and Cuban exile groups.

Summer 1960. Several clandestine stations and CIA-funded licensed stations in the United States joined Radio Swan in broadcasting to Cuba. Also the CIA-backed Cuban Freedom Committee produced "Free Cuba Radio," which recorded anti-Castro programs aired on licensed stations in the United States and abroad.

September 26, 1960. Castro protested Radio Swan before the United Nations.

October 1960. Cuba began operating La Voz de INRA (Instituto Nacional de Reforma Agraria), on the same frequency as Radio Swan, in order to block the latter's signal.

1961. CMCA, "The Friendly Voice of Cuba," began broadcasting to the United States and the Caribbean on medium-wave.

January 3, 1961. The United States broke diplomatic relations with Cuba.

February 1961. VOA prepared a series of anti-Castro programs directed at the Caribbean, including the one-hour documentary "Anatomy of a Broken Promise."

February 1961. Cuba began experimental broadcasts of what was to become Radio Havana Cuba, the official Cuban government overseas service.

April 17, 1961. The CIA-sponsored invasion force landed at the Bay of Pigs. VOA stepped up its broadcasts in support of the exile army.

May 1, 1961. Radio Havana Cuba officially began broadcasting on four short-wave channels.

Late 1961. Radio Swan changed its name to Radio Americas. It continued to broadcast from the same facilities under CIA direction.

September 1962. President Kennedy ordered an expansion of Spanish-language broadcasting by VOA and sought $3 million in new congressional appropriations for U.S. broadcasting to counter Cuban broadcasting in the region.

October 1962. Cuba began broadcasting a program called "Radio Free Dixie" to the United States on short-wave and medium-wave. The primary announcer, a fugitive black activist from the United States, called on blacks to commit acts of violence and subversion.

October 22, 1962. President Kennedy went on television to demand that the Soviet Union remove its missiles from Cuba. His speech also was broadcast to Cuba by a special VOA radio network of nine commercial AM stations in the United States.

November 1, 1962. The National Security Council directed VOA to initiate medium-wave broadcasts to Cuba from Florida.

November 2, 1962. Acting director of the USIA Donald Wilson reported to President Kennedy in a classified memo on the progress in implementing medium-wave broadcasting to Cuba and on other "possible escalations in radio broadcasting." However, he noted that putting medium-wave stations on the air "may possibly involve violations of the (NARBA)."

November 4, 1962. Cuban interference with Miami-area commercial stations, carrying VOA programming to Cuba, was reported.

November 9, 1962. A U.S. navy, 50 Kw, medium-wave transmitter became operational on Sugarloaf Key in Florida. It was linked with the special VOA network and broadcast to Cuba on 1040 Khz under temporary presidential authority, but without FCC approval or ITU registration.

November 14, 1962. VOA's own 50 Kw, medium-wave transmitter on Marathon Key began broadcasting to Cuba on 1180 Khz without FCC approval or ITU registration. USIA "released" the commercial U.S. stations that had been relaying VOA programs to Cuba. However, the USIA reported to the president that it was "still using the time some of these stations were previously selling to Cuban refugee groups in order to keep the exiles off the air."

December 3, 1962. USIA director Edward R. Murrow reported to President Kennedy in a secret memo that two U.S. military aircraft had been equipped for telecasting to Cuba. However, Murrow reported that the airborne television transmitters could be easily jammed and recommended that they should be used only as a "tactical weapon" under "the most grave and impelling circumstances." The airborne transmitters were under the command of General Edward Lansdale as part of Operation Mongoose, the covert CIA campaign against Cuba during the 1960s. General Lansdale gained considerable notoriety as the top U.S. psychological warfare specialist during the Huk rebellion in the Philippines in the 1950s and in Vietnam in the 1960s.

December 1962. As the missile crisis waned, VOA cut back its Cuban programming from twenty-four hours per day to only eight hours. President Kennedy gave special commendations to each of the commercial stations that had participated in the VOA emergency network.

February 25, 1963. Radio Liberty, a covertly funded CIA station located in Europe and directed at the Soviet Union, began relaying its programming in Russian to Soviet personnel stationed in Cuba via WBT, a 50 Kw, medium-wave commercial station in Charlotte, North Carolina.

Summer 1963. Using Soviet-supplied equipment, Cuba became the first nation in the Western Hemisphere to jam radio broadcasts. The first apparent target of the jamming was Russian-language programming from the United States.

1964. Cuba installed high-powered, Czech-built transmitters, without directional antennas, and U.S. stations, especially WGN on 720 Khz from Chicago, began to suffer serious interference from the new Cuban stations.

April 14, 1964. Cuban jammers were reported on six AM frequencies: 710, used by WGBS, a prominent Spanish-language station in Miami; 1040, used by the U.S. navy transmitter directed at Cuba; 1140, WMIE, Miami; 1160, used by the CIA's Radio Americas from Swan Island; 1180, VOA Marathon; and 1600, WKWF, Key West. All three Florida commercial stations participated in the special VOA network during the missile crisis, and WGBS and WKWF aired CIA-backed, Free Cuba Radio programs prior to the Bay of Pigs.

1965. Radio Free Dixie went off the air.

September 1965. The VOA relay via the U.S. navy transmitter in Florida was discontinued after the antenna was destroyed in a hurricane.

December 17 and 21, 1966. Officials of the FCC, USIA, National Security Council, State Department, and the Office of Telecommunications Management of the White House met to discuss the complaint of WHAM in Rochester, New York. The radio station was licensed by the FCC to operate on 1180 Khz, the same frequency used by VOA Marathon to broadcast to Cuba without FCC approval or

ITU registration. WHAM complained that it was experiencing interference from VOA Marathon and/or the Cuban jammer on 1180 Khz. In declassified minutes obtained under the Freedom of Information Act, a FCC representative noted that VOA Marathon was the first instance in which the United States had operated a medium-wave radio station, intended for foreign audiences from the continental United States and that the station was in violation of NARBA. The FCC questioned whether the continued operation of the Marathon station, which had been initiated with special presidential approval as an emergency measure during the missile crisis, could still be justified, and argued that its continued operation might endanger clear-channel service in the United States and complicate radio negotiations with other countries, such as Mexico. The State Department representative regarded continued VOA broadcasts to Cuba as "most important," despite the original rationale for the Marathon station. The USIA representative stated that "Marathon would probably be the last case for the use of medium-wave in the Americas." The FCC "reluctantly agree(d) to a six-month extension of Marathon's current operation on 1180 Kc/s, subject to the condition that a thorough examination of the problem be made during that time period."

April 1967. A FCC official warned in a speech before a radio broadcasters association that "interference danger in new Cuban superpower transmitters is real, present, and without ready solution." Cuba was reported to be installing six superpower Czech transmitters that could seriously disrupt U.S. commercial broadcasting. The industry group petitioned the U.S. government to seek a solution to the impending problem.

January 8, 1968. Radio Havana Cuba began relaying English-language "Voice of (North) Vietnam" programs on short-wave to the United States.

May 15, 1968. Radio Americas went off the air.

August 24, 1969. *The New York Times* reported that "Cuba appears to have toned down her powerful radio propaganda, which is directed at four continents in eight languages." It said that Havana broadcasting "is still strongly and consistently anti-United States. . . . But since the beginning of the year, the previously shrill and abrasive tone seems to have been gradually eliminated from Cuban foreign broadcasts."

1972. Anti-Castro clandestine stations operating mostly from southern Florida returned to the air in greater numbers. These unlicensed stations, sponsored primarily by Cuban exile groups, had been mostly silent since the early 1960s.

August 1, 1973. The FCC again attempted to gain control of the frequency assignment for VOA Marathon. In a letter to the White

House Office of Telecommunications Policy, the FCC chief engineer questioned the "USIA justification for the protracted operation of the Marathon station long since the end of the Cuban missile crisis." He also noted that the continued interference to WHAM, the radio station licensed to use 1180 Khz, indicated that the succession of short temporary approvals of the station by the White House should be discontinued, and the matter should be referred to the commission "for formal consideration and appropriate action."

April 1, 1973.   "Cita Con Cuba," a VOA Marathon program tailored for Cuban audiences by a predominately Cuban exile staff, was cut from five hours to a half hour.

December 1, 1974.   The remaining half hour of "Cita Con Cuba" was phased out, and the Marathon station continued to broadcast only generic VOA programming to Cuba.

January 8, 1976.   Radio Havana Cuba stopped relaying "Voice of Vietnam" to the United States.

December 1979.   The Cuban government formally notified the ITU of its intent to make large-scale additions to its medium-wave inventory. The Cuban plan included two 500 Kw transmitters.

February 1980.   "La Voz de Cuba" replaced its Spanish-language programming with English-language programming intended "for listeners in North America and the Caribbean." The Cuban, medium-wave channel (600 Khz) also relayed Radio Moscow's English-language programs.

February 7, 1980.   The FCC launched a new campaign to close down unlicensed anti-Castro stations operating from Florida. Commission agents targeted one of the most notorious clandestine broadcasters known as Commander David and closed down his plant near Miami.

March 1980.   Cuba and the United States attended the first session of the ITU Region II conference on medium-wave broadcasting. The meeting held in Buenos Aires established technical criteria upon which frequencies would be assigned at a second session in Rio de Janeiro. A U.S.-backed proposal for 9 Khz spacing was tabled until the second session.

June 16, 1980.   Senator Jesse Helms introduced a congressional resolution supportive of radio broadcasting to Cuba.

November 1980.   Cuba gave a one-year notice that it was withdrawing from NARBA.

1981.   The FCC registered the VOA Marathon station with the International Frequency Registration Board of the ITU for the first time.

April 6–7, 1981.   U.S. State Department and FCC negotiators met with Cuban officials in Havana to resolve bilateral differences prior to the next Region II session in Rio. A declassified State Department cable reporting on the meeting made the following major points: Discussions were "cordial but frank;" Cuba did not intend to use directional antennas to resolve incompatibilities—too expensive; Cuba saw 9 Khz spacing as the only solution; Cuba vigorously complained about the use of medium-wave for propaganda against it (that is, VOA Marathon and Radio Swan); the Cuban representatives said they had not asked the United States to delete the Marathon station from its inventory and, therefore, did not expect the United States to ask them not to install their two 500 Kw stations; the Cubans added: "These stations are only to counter Marathon. Just as the U.S. wants its friends in Cuba to be able to listen to Marathon, Cuba wants its friends in U.S. to be able to listen to Cuban stations."

April 14, 1981. In a major test case, the U.S. Justice Department refused to prosecute Commander David, the celebrated anti-Castro broadcaster, charged by the FCC with operating a clandestine station from southern Florida. FCC officials complained that, despite solid evidence against Commander David, the case was dropped for "political reasons." An increase in clandestine activity by anti-Castro broadcasters immediately followed the dismissal.

July 15, 1981. The Central Committee and Ministry of Communications announced that Cuba intended to spend a large amount of money on international broadcasting during the coming five-year period.

August 24–28, 1981. U.S.-Cuban bilateral talks on radio interference continued in Washington.

August 27, 1981. *The New York Times* reported that the Reagan administration planned to launch Radio Martí.

September 17, 1981. Wayne S. Smith, head of the U.S. Interests Section in Havana, cabled the State Department that a U.S. decision to proceed with Radio Martí "could well destroy any progress on resolving AM broadcasting incompatibilities."

September 22, 1981. President Reagan officially announced plans to start Radio Martí.

October 14, 1981. The U.S. Interests Section in Havana dissented on the plan to establish Radio Martí.

October 26, 1981. President Castro, in a speech in Havana, said: "The imperialists will multiply their subversive activities and in recent days with the greatest possible gall and cynicism they announced they are going to establish an official radio station of the United States government directed against the Cuban Revolution. You have to be quite cynical and immoral and shameless to speak of establishing a radio station on U.S. soil to campaign against the Revolution, to try to destabilize and subvert the Revolution. You must be cynical, very cynical! There is no more vulgar and brutal form of intervention in the internal affairs of a country. . . . Of course, there will be a response to that measure. . . ."

November 1981. A variety of other Cuban officials threatened to retaliate if the United States broadcast to Cuba.

November 9, 1981. The second session of the Region II MF Conference began in Rio.

December 7, 1981. Cuba began to shift to its new, unapproved inventory of AM stations.

December 14, 1981. Cuba withdrew from the Rio conference, citing U.S. plans "to set up medium-wave transmitters beamed exclusively at our country for subversive, destabilizing purposes. . . ."

Late 1981. Cuba stopped relaying Radio Moscow's English-language service on AM.

February 6, 1982. A declassified cable from the CIA reported that satellite photography of Cuba showed that an anti-aircraft artillery emplacement had been built near a new antenna probably intended to counter Radio Martí.

February 9, 1982. The U.S. Interests Section in Havana reported that Cuba "will pull out all stops in retaliation to Radio Martí," including establishing a counter-broadcasting station named Radio Lincoln.

March 12, 1982. The International Frequency Registration Board of the ITU seemingly accepted Cuba's changes in its AM radio inventory. Those changes previously had been blocked by the United States at the Rio conference.

April 4, 1982. Describing Cubans as "boxers waiting to go into the ring," President Castro again promised retaliation if Radio Martí went on the air.

August 19, 1982. In answering questions of U.S. journalists about the Cuban response to Radio Martí, President Castro said: "We are not going to interfere, but we are going to broadcast back; I think the Americans are going to be listening to a lot of Cuban music."

August 30, 1982. "The Voice of Cuba" interfered with U.S. broadcasters as a "test and demonstration" of Cuba's ability to respond to Radio Martí.

November 8, 1982. Cuba protested U.S. plans for Radio Martí before the ITU Plenipotentiary Conference in Nairobi.

March 4, 1983. After meeting with State Department officials, representatives of the National Association of Broadcasters announced their opposition to Radio Martí on the grounds that it would use an AM frequency and might provoke a radio war with Cuba.

May 20, 1983. In a speech before the Cuban American National

Foundation in Miami, President Reagan strongly supported Radio Martí and lavished praise on Jorge Mas Canosa (chairman of the foundation, former broadcaster on the CIA's Radio Swan, Bay of Pigs veteran, member of the President's Commission on Broadcasting to Cuba, and leading anti-Castro activist in Miami).

August 8–9, 1983.   The United States and Cuba held secret talks in Costa Rica in an attempt to resolve the radio interference issue.

October 4, 1983.   President Reagan signed Public Law 98-111, establishing Radio Martí.

May 20, 1985.   Radio Martí began broadcasting.   Cuba suspended an important immigration agreement with the United States but did not immediately counter-broadcast or further interfere with U.S. stations.

May 20, 1985.   FCC formally requested the International Frequency Registration Board to investigate Cuban stations operating at variance with their inventories.

September 20, 1985.   For the first time since Radio Martí went on the air, President Castro threatened Cuban broadcast retaliation: "We have powerful radio stations. . . . They existed before.   They are weapons we have here because they are threatening us with subversive radio. We have very powerful stations! Both medium-wave and short-wave. Let me tell you that by putting some equipment together we can get together 1000 Kilowatts, not 50 or 100. If we turn on these stations, radio will not be heard again in the United States."

October 23, 1985.   WAQI Radio Mambí (710 Khz), a Spanish-language station in Miami, went on the air boasting that it would broadcast anti-Castro programming to Cuba. Some station officials said that they were disappointed that Radio Martí was not sufficiently strident and hoped to fill the gap. The station was created from a merger with WQBA (formerly WMIE), a station that cooperated with the CIA and VOA in broadcasting to Cuba in the early 1960s.

October 26, 1985.   Radio Mambí reportedly was heavily jammed from Cuba.

November 3, 1985.   Radio Taino, an English- and Spanish-language station from Havana, went on the air. However, it broadcast only at low power during the day minimizing interference to U.S. stations.

December 13, 1985.   The FCC filed a formal complaint with the Cuban government charging Cuban interference with U.S. stations.

February 4, 1986.   President Castro again attacked Radio Martí in a speech before the Third Party Congress in Havana.

February 10, 1986.   Radio Martí increased its daily programming three hours to a total of seventeen and a half hours, daily.

May 1986.   Members of ITU Region II met in Geneva. A second meeting was scheduled. Cuba continued to protest Radio Martí.

July 8–9, 1986.   U.S. and Cuban negotiators met in Mexico City to discuss the possible resurrection of the immigration agreement suspended by Cuba in retaliation for Radio Martí. The talks collapsed after the United States refused to grant Cuba clear-channel access to the U.S. AM radio band to match Radio Martí broadcasts to Cuba.

October 5, 1986.   "Diversionary propaganda against Cuba" was among the topics discussed by Soviet Foreign Minister Shevardnadze and President Castro during their talks in Havana.

October 11, 1986.   At the Iceland summit, President Reagan complained about Soviet jamming of Voice of America.   Secretary Gorbachev reportedly answered: "We shall stop jamming the Voice of America and you shall give us the opportunity on your territory or somewhere nearby of setting up radio broadcasts to the United States so that they will get through to the population of your country."

December 2, 1986.   A Cuban station operating on 1160 AM broadcast at high power an evening speech of Fidel Castro, causing interference to U.S. broadcasters.

May 1987.   According to testimony at the Iran-*contra* hearings, Lt. Col. Oliver North diverted proceeds from secret arms sales to purchase broadcasting equipment for a clandestine station directed at Cuba. North reportedly became impatient with the delays in establishing Radio Martí and sought to start secret broadcasts from an unnamed Caribbean island. However, the plan was never implemented.

May 23, 1987.   Radio Moscow's English-language service began broadcasting on 1040 AM from a powerful transmitter in Cuba. These new broadcasts coincided with an end of Russian jamming of VOA broadcasts to the Soviet Union. Although operating at relatively high power, the Radio Moscow broadcasts were on the air only during weekend days, causing only minor interference to two Florida stations. Nonetheless, the U.S. State Department protested to Havana and Moscow saying that "such broadcasting contravenes International Telecommunication Union regulations."

INDEX

Afghanistan, 10-11
Africa, 61; Cuban aid, 41-42, 49-50; Cuban military, 37-38; Cuba's role, 36-45, 47, 48; unity, 48-49. *See also various countries*
African National Congress (ANC), 48
Agrarian Reform Act (1959) (Cuba), 70, 78, 85-86
Aid, 65; to Africa, 41-42, 46(n7), 49; Cuban, 28, 37, 41-42, 49-50; education, 49-50; United States, 32, 37, 89
Aircraft: in Cuba, 8, 117-118; Soviet, 3-4, 116, 117; United States, 121, 122, 147-148. *See also* Airspace; Military
Airspace: Cuban, 113-115; Cuban security, 115-118; U.S. violations, 114, 115, 118, 121-122
Algeria, 37
ANC. *See* African National Congress
Angola, 55-57; Cuban aid, 5, 36, 37, 40-41, 42, 43, 46(n7); Cuban troops, 37-38, 45, 51-52, 54; South African invasion, 53, 55; U.S. policy, 36, 40-41, 43, 54, 92
Anti-communism, 18
Apartheid, 52-53, 55, 57
Argentina, 27, 91
Arias plan, 17-18, 22, 32
Asia, 61
Assassination attempts, 104, 111
Assets, 91
Assistance. *See* Aid

Bahamas, 31
Barbados, 31
Barre, Mohammad Siad, 38, 51
Batista, Fulgencio, 30
Bay of Pigs invasion, 127, 146
Belgian Congo, 37. *See also* Zaire
Belize, 27
Bilirakis, Michael, 104
Bipartisan Commission Report on Central America, 32, 33
Blockade: United States, 31-32, 89, 90-91, 94. *See also* Embargo
Botha, Pieter, 53
Botswana, 54
Broadcasting, 141, 143, 150-151; agreements, 125-126, 136(n7); Cuban, 128, 129, 138-139, 142, 146; interference, 124-125, 128-129, 130-134, 135(n3), 143, 148-149, 151-152, 154; transmitters, 140-142; United States, 142-143, 145-146, 147-148; U.S. propaganda, 127-130, 139-142, 148-150. *See also various broadcasts; radio stations*

Canada, 31

Caribbean: Cuban policy, 21-23, 24, 27-30, 31. *See also individual countries*
Carter administration: Angola, 41, 44; Cuban relations, 25, 29, 92; Nicaragua, 15, 16; U.S. security, 117-118
Casablanca Group, 48, 49
Castro, Fidel, 21, 80, 104, 245; Latin American policy, 27, 29
Central America, 17, 32; U.S. objectives, 14-21. *See also* Caribbean; Latin America
Central Intelligence Agency (CIA), 104, 115; in Nicaragua, 18-19; radio broadcasting, 127, 139, 146, 147-148
Cerezo, Vinicio, 20
CIA. *See* Central Intelligence Agency
Cienfuegos: naval base, 3, 101
Civil defense, 105
Coca-Cola, 94
Colonialism: in Africa, 48; in Latin America, 27, 30
Communications Ministry (Cuba), 138
Companies. *See* Corporations
Congo-Brazzaville, 37, 49
Constitution of the Republic of Cuba, 26, 30, 33(nn1, 2)
Constructive engagement: Reagan administration, 52, 54, 55
Contadora process, 17, 19, 21, 32
Contras: U.S. support, 17, 19, 23, 32
Corporations, 92; certificates, 76-77; nationalization compensation claims, 70-71, 83, 93, 94-95; normalization, 73-74, 75; tax credits, 75-76
Counter-revolutionary activities, 104-105. *See also* Covert activities
Covert activities: CIA, 18-19, 104, 115, 127, 139, 146, 147-148
Cuba, 59, 90; African relations, 44-45, 47, 48-49; airspace threats, 113-118; Angola, 37-38, 40-41, 42, 43, 51-52; broadcasting, 126, 132-133, 134, 135(n3), 151-152, 153; defense, 116, 117; dependency, 47-48; foreign policy, 5-6, 10-11, 25-26; Guantánamo Base, 108, 110-111; Horn of Africa, 38-49, 51-52; Latin American policy, 21-23, 24, 26-30; military assistance, 51-52; nationalization, 69-71, 73-74, 75-76; non-alignment, 11-13; Sandinista support, 16, 17, 19, 20-22; security agenda, 103-106; South African policy, 53, 54, 55-57; Soviet aid, 65, 78-79; Soviet relations, 1-2, 3-4, 6-7, 8, 9, 25; trade, 90-91; in United Nations, 58, 59, 61, 64-65, 66; United States as threat, 6, 7-8, 12; U.S. embargo, 79-81; U.S. relations, 25, 30, 59, 87-88, 89, 92, 94-95,

155

156   *Index*